A Little Handbook of Stratigraphic Exercises:
Mastering the Harris Matrix

A Little Handbook of Stratigraphic Exercises

Mastering the Harris Matrix

Adonice-Ackad Baaklini

ARCHAEOPRESS ARCHAEOLOGY

Archaeopress Publishing Ltd
13-14 Market Square
Bicester
Oxfordshire OX26 6AD
United Kingdom

www.archaeopress.com

ISBN 978-1-80583-227-0
ISBN 978-1-80583-228-7 (e-Pdf)

This book is available direct from Archaeopress or from our website www.archaeopress.com

I dedicate this book to my family.

CONTENTS

CHAPTER 3. EXPLANATIONS AND COMMENTS ON THE EXERCISES 31

LIST OF FIGURES

FOREWORD

This is an excellent book for the field archaeologist on the most important parts of the archaeological process which is of excavation and recording.

Stratigraphy and excavation by layers of datable deposits is the key to the door of understanding a site and the recording of artefacts and deposits with unique codes, drawings and photography is essential to the post-excavation work of recording and dating a site.

A site can be a simple deposition or can be more complex with later intrusive features as postholes or pits and in some cases burials cut into earlier deposits.

The understanding and dating of a site can only be achieved by due process and this book is essential to explain that process and is to be recommended to all archaeologists.

Dr Paul Wilkinson MCIfA., FRSA

HOW TO USE THIS BOOK

This book falls conveniently into three chapters: Introduction, Exercises, and Explanations.

Chapter 1 focuses on the presentation of the Harris matrix and the concepts and tools needed to understand it, while Chapter 2 offers 25 stratigraphy exercises. The latter are organised by degree of difficulty, from easiest to hardest, and centre on the creation of Harris matrices based on a drawing of a section from an imaginary site with the stratigraphic units highlighted. The exercises are resolved in Chapter 3 (Explanations) with comments on the salient points.

Chapter 1 is by no means exhaustive but is rather intended to give the reader the basic understanding necessary to start creating matrices. The concept of Chapter 1 will be explained within the context of each example as we go along – there is no need to memorise or fully understand the basics from the first read.

The exercises that make up Chapters 2 and 3 need really to be taken in isolation: it is highly recommended you check the explanations after each exercise, and not wait until you have finished a group of them. The comments in Chapter 3 will often refer to the theories in Chapter 1, so hopping from Chapters 3 to 1 will become a natural thing to do.

Paper and a pen are all you need to tackle the exercises, but the geeks among you could, of course, use any design software.

CHAPTER 1.
INTRODUCTION

Before starting with the exercises and creating your own matrices, Chapter 1 will give you everything you need to know about how to build a good one. You will learn what stratigraphy is, what the stratigraphic rules are, how stratigraphy is divided by units, and, eventually, how a matrix is built.

1. What is archaeological stratigraphy?

Understanding stratigraphy is the key to any successful excavation. This section will define archaeological stratigraphy and its development over the last two centuries.

1a. General definition

Archaeological stratigraphy basically designates everything related to the different layers and features encountered during an excavation. The term stratigraphy was not invented by archaeologists but by geologists, appearing at the beginning of the 19th century in studies seeking to distinguish different geological strata, and, especially, to divide them up according to the fossils they contained – as an example we can cite the work of William Smith (Smith 1816). It became a logical step to transfer this notion of stratigraphy to archaeology, involving as it does the identification and study of strata.

For archaeology, by contrast, the different strata are not only 'natural' but 'anthropic'. Schiffer (1987: 7) gives a concise and clear summary of these two main concepts in the formation process of stratification in archaeology, i.e. 'Formation processes are of two basic kinds: cultural, where the agency of transformation is human behavior; and non-cultural, in which the agencies stem from processes of the natural environment'.

In a more practical way, this means that archaeologists have to study the natural and anthropic actions that changed any given area. Basically, these actions consist of adding or removing/moving material. Let's look at some examples. Natural phenomena, like natural sand accumulation, will add material and create a layer, while floods can remove earth and even destroy human constructions; people adding earth to an uneven surface to level it will add material and create an anthropic layer; the same will happen at every scale, when constructing a skyscraper, for example, and, conversely, by digging a pit for rubbish they will remove material; likewise, during a siege, Roman soldiers would remove material when they destroyed walls with their battering rams. In addition, in this last example, material was not only removed from its original place, but also moved to another area: i.e. we find collapsed remains from the wall at its base.

It is worth making a distinction here between 'stratification', which is the phenomenon, and 'stratigraphy', which is the study of the phenomenon of stratification.

1b. History

We can distinguish three main phases in the evolution of stratigraphy in archaeology: 1) the first when 'diggers' began to observe stratification and comment on the different strata they removed; 2) the phase during which the excavation practice was intended to remove the deposits layer by layer, and not just assess the stratification at the end of the excavation; 3) and a third phase, characterised by the invention of the stratigraphic matrix by British archaeologist E.C. Harris, the most powerful tool yet for displaying the stratigraphy of any given site.

If some early 'diggers', including Thomas Jefferson (the US president) and Meadows Taylor, are usually quoted as the first to attempt to introduce a scientific method into excavations, the real beginning of stratigraphy, and then of archaeological excavations, began in the last decades of the 19th century, as, gradually, more and more excavators stopped just removing soil to reach structures without commenting on what they were removing. This first phase is characterised by the observation of stratigraphy in sections at the end of the dig, i.e. 'post facto stratigraphic' observation (Browman and Givens 1996: 81). Some excavators produced sketches of their sections and then started to divide their strata. Stratigraphy was born. (We must note that trying to identify the person responsible for the first such project is difficult, and also not very useful. Obviously it was a collaborative and shared work by archaeologists of the time.)

The second phase, from the beginning of the 20th century, involved an important shift – instead of just observing and commenting on the stratification in section at the end of an excavation, some archaeologists began to remove the deposit based on their stratigraphic analyses. At that time, the idea of digging 'layer by layer' preoccupied several archaeologists. During the first couple of decades of the 20th century, two main schools of excavation appeared, i.e. one based on excavating strata as they are (the natural stratigraphy), and the other based on artificial layers. The Mexican, Manuel Gamio, trained by the American School of Mexico, then linked to Columbia University, may have been one of the first to excavate partially by 'natural' layers (Gamio 1913: 180–181, 187, fig. 2). Niels C. Nelson, an American archaeologist, was one of the first to promote the removal of deposits methodically, i.e. via his early article, 'Chronology of the Tano Ruins, New Mexico', where he explains making regular (50 cm) artificial layers (Nelson 1916). If this method might seem strange to us, it is worth noting that within the context of American archaeology in specific regions, with very homogeneous layers, this is more 'understandable', with this method intending to make a study of material concentrations through equal units. Just one year later, Alfred Kidder published the first article with a clear written mention of excavation by actual layers (Kidder and Kidder 1917: 340).

These archaeologists just quoted, we must remember, were not alone in their 'discovery': they were actively communicating with colleagues in America and Europe. It is very possible, therefore, that stratigraphic excavations were undertaken before them, or were theorised in part by others. Indeed, during the same period, other excavators referred to strata and layers in their reports, but it is not always easy to know if they were analysing these after their work, or if they had also adopted the layer-by-layer method. At that time, indeed, methodological issues about excavation were not always developed by archaeologists – at least in their published reports.

This second phase culminated with two well-known British archaeologists who made the layer-by-layer method common – Mortimer Wheeler (1954) and Kathleen Kenyon (1961). These researchers developed specific field methods for recording strata and remains in that way. Most of what they wrote is still applicable, with the exception of their idea that the archaeologist should interpret the layer on the ground, a theory that clearly introduces a bias in recording and excavating; nowadays almost all archaeologists agree that neutrality in recording is indispensable for good archaeological data recovery and more accurate interpretation later.

The third phase corresponds to the invention of the Harris matrix, which put stratigraphy at the centre of archaeological recording. The inventor was E.C. Harris, a British archaeologist in 1973, who then published the principle in 1975 (Harris 1975). Based on his concept, the most important question when excavating was no longer 'what is it?', but 'what is above what, and what is below what?'. This is an important shift, because if, from a good drawing or photograph, we can always refine the interpretation of a structure, a 'bad' excavation, i.e. missing the stratification, can never be corrected in the future. Furthermore, in addition to removing the archaeology 'layer by layer', it must be removed in the right order, i.e. the latest layer first – although this ideal scenario is not always possible due to field constraints and strategy. This is why, while excavating, stratigraphy has to be the focal point of the archaeologist who is handling the trowel: only they can reveal the stratigraphy. All the other questions, i.e. chronology, interpretations, etc., can be answered by many specialists now, one, ten, or even 100 years later.

2. The rules of stratigraphy

The following rules, usually quoted in field archaeology manuals, are general ones that can explain significant elements of archaeological deposits. Of course, there will be many caveats, but bearing these rules in mind – with their exceptions – will help archaeologists on the ground analyse what they have in front of their eyes.

2a. Superposition

This rule states that layers are deposited one above the other, from earliest to latest. In other words, the highest deposits should be later than the lowest ones. In a general manner this works well, and it is at the base of stratigraphic observation. Yet, it is obvious there will be exceptions, and most of these are presented in Chapter 2 (Exercises).

2b. Original horizontality

According to this rule, the majority of deposits tend to become horizontal over time. You can verify this by throwing buckets of earth: if at the beginning you have a small 'hill' in the middle, several hours later the deposit will start to have a horizontal form, with slimmed-down edges. This holds true in an open field, and is altered by the 'basin of deposition' of the layer. This notion of basin of deposition is very important in archaeology, because it will determine the way the layers were deposited. For example, the fill of a rubbish pit has the pit's cut as a basin of deposition; or the natural sand accumulation inside an abandoned house has the wall of the house as a basin of deposition. In theory, each layer will have a basin of deposition, but not all will constrain and influence its form as in the two previous examples. And this is what is important in the field – to identify any constraining basin of deposition and to understand how it influenced the deposition process. An aeolian deposit in the bottom of a canyon will have the terrace and bedrock slope as a basin, the same aeolian deposit in a desert could have an infinite zone as a basin of deposition, but at this scale this is no longer relevant for archaeology, or even geology.

2c. Original continuity

This rule states that the layers deposited should be continuous, and constitute one unit, unless a specific action separated or removed them. This means that if your deposit suddenly has a vertical edge without being constrained by any basin of deposition, we should wonder why. Indeed, naturally it should have had slimmed-down edges, and yet it can be standing vertically like that – try to deposit your previous earth experiment into a cube shape... This often happens when you have any kind of cut in the ground. Let's take the case of a long medieval ditch interrupting the deposit around it. It will also be crucial to consider if this discontinuing layer has a continuity somewhere, on the other side of the ditch, for example. In such a case, the two deposits on both sides of the ditch were originally the same. These two layers will have to be recorded separately, but we will link them by a 'same as' link to acknowledge their original state.

2d. Stratigraphic succession

This precept is the key notion to the Harris matrix. It states that if on the ground the archaeologist is always trying to see what layer is above what, and as such studying the physical relation between the layers, the final goal of stratigraphy is not only to know what is above what, but also to know what is chronologically later than what. The result of this analysis provides the base for building any effective relative chronology. Then, the archaeologist has to separate physical and stratigraphic links. On the matrix, priority has to be given to stratigraphic links. This rule seems the most 'incomprehensible' for newcomers to the stratigraphic method, but patience – everything will become clear later, and with the exercises. For now, just memorise this:

'The stratigraphic matrix is a tool to build a chronology of your stratigraphic units, not to know which units "touch" which.'

3. Stratigraphic units (SU)

Before going to the stratigraphic matrix itself, let's take a look at the 'raw material' of the matrix: the stratigraphic unit.

3a. General definition

The stratigraphic unit or context – as it is referred to by UK-trained/influenced archaeologists – is the smallest division that can be made in archaeology. The 'layer-by-layer' excavation talked about by early 20th-century archaeologists finds its best parallel in the Stratigraphic Unit system. The Harris matrix aims to arrange these SUs according to the rule of stratigraphic succession. Apart from very limited cases, e.g. artificial layers, an SU should be a reflection of what the archaeologist sees on the ground.

A simple way to define the SU is to think of the following equation: 1 SU = 1 action. This action could be momentary (e.g. a wall collapse) or long-lasting (e.g. an aeolian sand deposit forming over decades or more). It is important to note that we can also divide a general main action into a series of events. Take the example of the building of a wall, where its construction can be divided into: 1) the excavation of a foundation trench; 2) the construction of the foundation wall inside the trench; 3) the construction of the wall itself. These three events have to be allocated different SUs (i.e. for the wall, for the foundation wall, for the foundation cut). It makes no difference whether these actions took place on the same day or not.

3b. The different kinds of SU

There are three main kinds of SU:

1. The deposit. This is the most popular, being described as any deposition of sediment: a natural accumulation of earth, a man-made levelling layer, the infiltration sediment inside a tomb, etc.
2. The cut. This includes any cut made in the sediment: a pit dug for refuse, a posthole, a foundation trench, etc.
3. Masonry. Here we record any 'masoned' element, as varied as a dry-laid and randomly arranged low dividing wall, a Roman temple, or a traditional Malian mud mosque.

As well as these three main categories, a further, specific kind of SU is used to record skeletal remains. Here the most important thing for us is not how skeletons are recorded, but only that a skeleton is itself an SU. In general, when possible, archaeologists will allocate one SU for each individual.

Another type of SU, not commonly used during excavations, is the SBU (stratigraphic building unit), employed by building archaeologists to understand the different phases of a construction by studying its elevation. It is mainly based on the analysis of the facade of a wall. Exercise 25 shows an example of how SBUs can also be classified using the Harris matrix.

SUs are also very occasionally preferred by specialists studying rock art, with each layer of drawing/engraving given an SU number and then all the layers arranged in a matrix to show how they relate. This adoption of SUs by art historians is proof of how useful and powerful SUs and the Harris matrix can be.

Some archaeologists like to group SUs into structures or features, e.g. the cut and the fill of a pit will be grouped within a feature number – SU 1 fill and SU 2 cut = feature 1 posthole. This method is very helpful in a context where the architecture incorporated mainly perishable elements, i.e. prehistoric and medieval sites across Europe, where archaeologists literally dig 'fields' of postholes. It is not a problem using this method for stratigraphy if each element of the structure is always recorded alone with a unique SU.

4. Analysing and presenting stratigraphy: the matrix

This section provides the basics of how to construct a Harris matrix for any archaeological site.

4a. The 'prehistory' of the stratigraphic matrix

The stratigraphic matrix did not appear from thin air in archaeology. Even if the Harris diagram looks unique, its notion – a snapshot of the stratigraphy in an easy-to-read visualisation – existed previously.

Edward Harris himself acknowledges that Kathleen Kenyon was the first to provide a diagram to show a correlation between layers and periodisation (Kenyon 1961: fig. 13). The diagram featured a section with labelled layers, and a table grouping the layers by period, with a short description of each. By this, Kenyon took a step further than archaeologists before her, who relied on making counts of the diagnostic material for each period by layer.

4b. The 'standard' matrix: the Harris matrix

The goal of the Harris matrix – or the stratigraphic diagram – is to present the stratigraphy of an area, or even a whole site, in an easy way, by focusing on the chronology. To do so, the stratigraphic units are arranged into a diagram and linked together according to their relations.

Let's start by looking at the relationships between the SUs that exist within the matrix. There are just three:

1. No direct relation. The SUs are not connected by any line on the matrix (Figure 1a).
2. Superimposition. SU 1 is above SU 2, or the other way around. The SUs are linked by a line (Figure 1b).
3. Correlation ('same as'). Two SUs that were initially one but were divided by a later action. The two SUs are connected by a horizontal double line (Figure 1c).

With the four rules in mind (see Chapter 1.2) and the three possible relationships between the SUs, you can start to build your matrix. It is a very logical system that can help deal with every situation in the field. Logically, the latest SU will be at the top of your diagram, and the earliest one at the bottom. The most common error by inexperienced (and even experienced) archaeologists is to fail to distinguish between stratigraphic relations and physical relations. We must keep in mind that, as archaeologists, our goal is to understand 'what is above what, but also to provide a chronology of the SUs'.

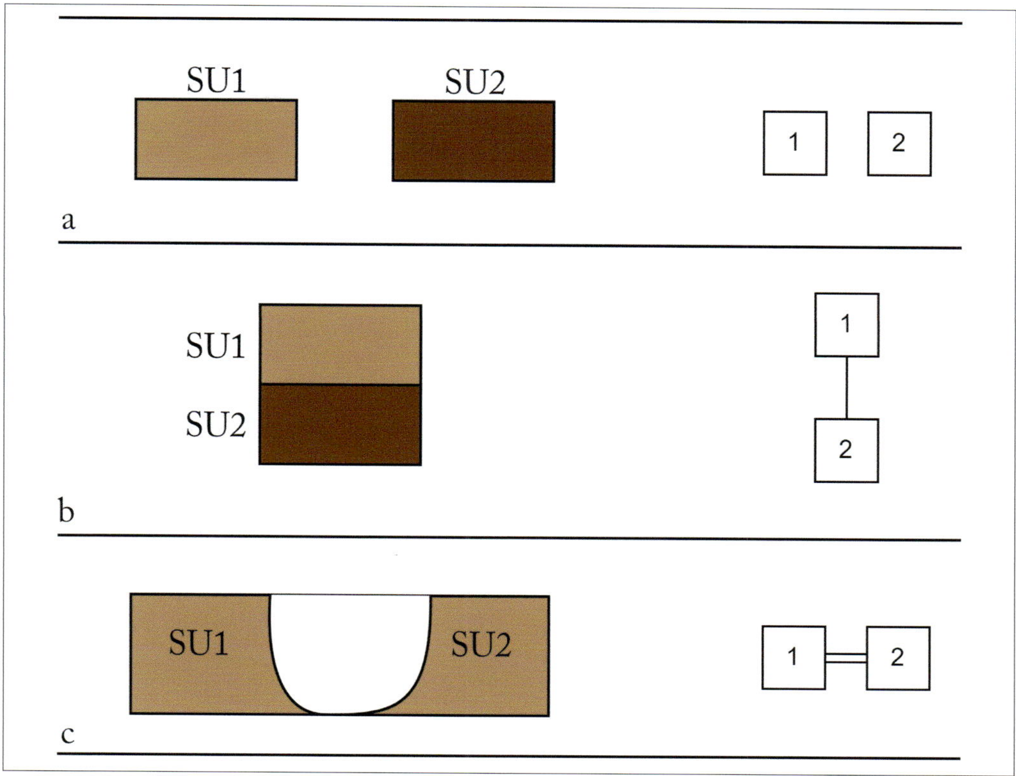

Figure 1: The different possible relationships between two stratigraphic units.

Let's take an example. SU 1 is above SU 2 and SU 3, but we do not have to show these physical relationships (as in Figure 2, diagram a). We have to understand the chronology. We see that SU 1 is flowing onto SU 2, and not the other way around. So SU 1 is later than SU 2, and SU 2 is later than SU 3. We only need to show these relations in the matrix (as you can see in Figure 2, diagram b).

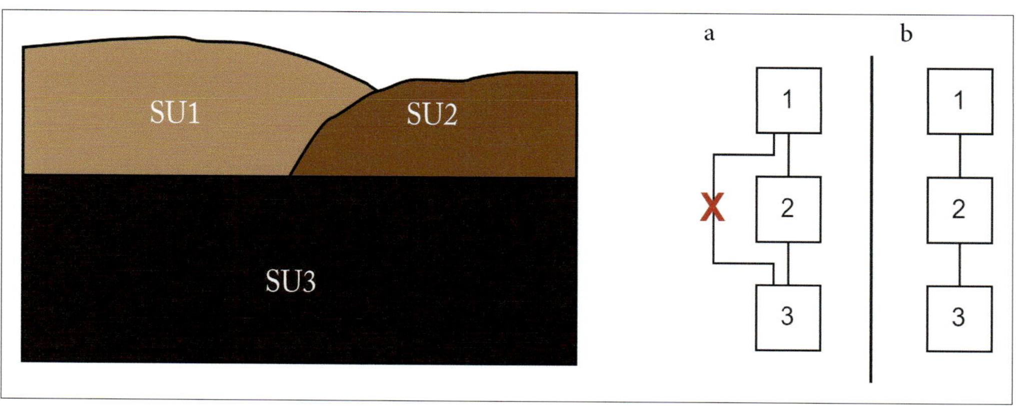

Figure 2: Physical versus stratigraphic relationships.

There you go then – you just need a notebook and something to write with and you can start to do your own matrix... in the field!

'In the field' – the phrase highlighted by Harris himself – and perhaps the most important words in this present book. A stratigraphic matrix should initially be made in the field – and, as we have seen, this is a very easy and obvious task towards helping you understand your stratigraphy on the ground. This is our job as archaeologists. Do not 'invert' the process – ascertain the stratigraphy *on the ground*, and then interpret your feature back at your desk (or even on site if you can). You can work on combining the matrices of different areas of your site, or work on phasing, as much as you want.

Phasing will be our next focus, but before moving further, keep in mind that every archaeologist, from senior to trainee, can create a matrix of what they are excavating, whether a small feature, an area, or the whole site. Do not believe those who say: 'Oh, that's too difficult for you now, you can try that later!' Don't be put off: the matrix – you can do it, and, actually, you must do it!

4c. Phasing the stratigraphic matrix

After composing your matrix with all the correct relationships, the next step will be to group your SUs by phase. This can be done easily by adding indications on the side of your diagram (Figure 3). The first step of the phasing is to give a relative phasing based on stratigraphy. Then, by reviewing the material and the typology of the feature, it is possible to give a definitive chronology.

It is key to think in terms of *groups of events* that create a common phase, and then, if you can, add the chronological markers: e.g. a group of postholes will be Phase I; the stone wall and foundations that cut this group will be Phase II; and then the abandonment layer – the collapsed building stones and the accumulation of natural sediments – constitute Phase III. Based on this, it will be very easy afterwards to add any chronological markers to these phases after analysing any

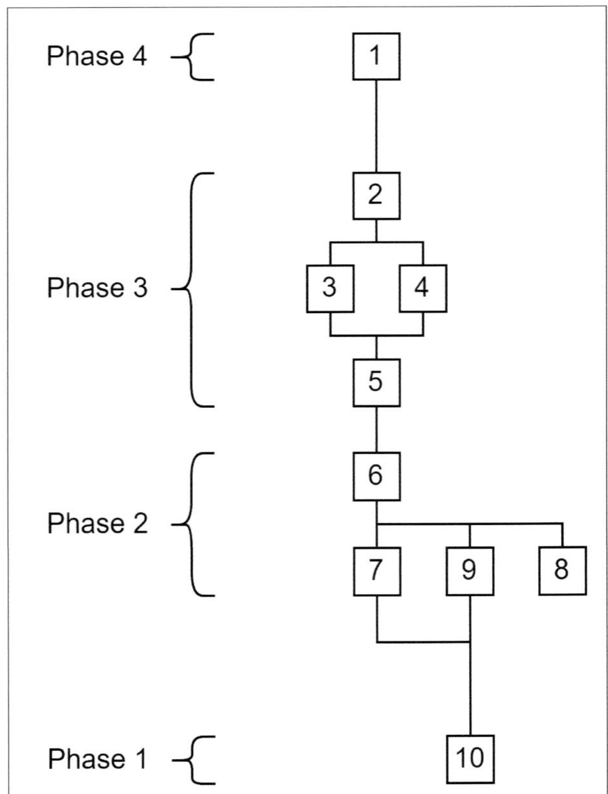

Figure 3: Example of a phased matrix.

artifacts and the structure, or following any possible archaeometrical investigations, i.e. C-14, OSL, dendrochronology, thermoluminescence, etc.

The final layout can then be a fully phased matrix, with attention even given to the vertical disposition of the SUs, with those clustered together being chronologically close.

4d. Other possibilities and developments

Several archaeologists have further refined the Harris system with indications about the types of SUs, i.e. adding functional information to the stratigraphy. It is important to remember that the goal of the matrix is primarily to show stratigraphic relationships, and any additional information should not obscure these.

The commonest indication added to matrices by archaeologists is the division between the cut and the deposit. For example, in a region where I have frequently worked, it is standard practice among the archaeologists of the General Directorate of Antiquities of Lebanon to signify deposits with circles and cuts with squares on their matrices (Figure 4). And at the famous 'Fischmarkt' site on Lake Constance, the highlighting of SU types on the diagrams was extensively employed, i.e. every earth layer, pit, fill, floor, etc. (Bibby 1993: 118–121). Further enhancements include specific contexts which prompt archaeologists to add specific legends to each SU number, showing, e.g., the presence/absence of material, especially ceramics (Orton 1980: 75, fig. 3.7).

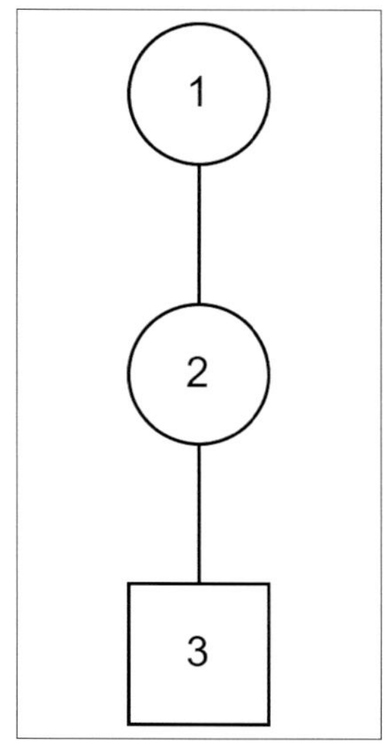

Figure 4: Example of a Beirut-style matrix.

5. References

Bibby, D.I. 1993. Building Stratigraphic Sequences on Excavations: an Example from Konstanz, Germany, in E.C. Harris, M.R. Brown and G.J. Brown (eds) *Practices of Archaeological Stratigraphy*: 104–121. London: Academic Press.

Browman, D.L. and D.R. Givens 1996. Stratigraphic Excavation: The First 'New Archaeology'. *American Anthropologist* 98(1): 80–95.

Gamio, M. 1913. Arqueologia de Atzcapotzalco, D.F. Mexico, in *XVIII International Congress of Americanists*: 180–187. London: Harrison and Sons.

Harris, E.C. 1975. The Stratigraphic Sequence: A Question of Time. *World Archaeology* 7(1): 109–121.

Kenyon, K. 1961. *Beginning in Archaeology*. London: Phoenix House.

Kidder V.A. and M.A. Kidder 1917. Notes on the Pottery of Pecos. *American Anthropologist* 19(3): 325–360.

Nelson, N.C. 1916. Chronology of the Tano Ruins, New Mexico. *American Anthropologist* 16(2): 159–180.

Orton, C. 1980. *Mathematics in Archaeology*. London: Collins.

Schiffer, M.B. 1987. *Formation Processes of the Archaeological Record*. Albuquerque: University of New Mexico Press.

Smith, W. 1816. *Strata Identified by Organized Fossils*. London: W. Arding.
Wheeler, M. 1954. *Archaeology from the Earth*. Oxford: Oxford University Press.

6. Selected bibliography (in chronological order, by most recent)

Ortega-Alvarado, L.M., Á.L. García-Fernández, F. Conde-Rodríguez and J.M. Jurado-Rodriguez 2022. Integrated and interactive 4D system for archaeological stratigraphy. *Archaeological and Anthropological Sciences* 14.203: 1–19.

- An article that includes an introduction to the various software available for the creation of stratigraphic matrices.

Gilento, P. 2020. Appendix: The Methods of Building Archaeology, in S. Anastasio *Building Between the two Rivers. An Introduction to the Building Archaeology of Ancient Mesopotamia*: 124–144. Oxford: Archaeopress.

- An introduction to building archaeology and the use of Stratigraphic Building Units (SBUs) and Harris matrices for built heritage.

Wilkinson, P. 2020. *Archaeology. What it is, where it is, and how to do it*. Oxford: Archaeopress.

- An indispensable companion to this present book for those seeking to master excavation methods, representing one of the most concise and modern works on the subject. It can be seen as an update to the famous MOLAS manual.

Kimball, J.L. 2016. *3D Delineation: A Modernisation of Drawing Methodology for Field Archaeology*. Oxford: Archaeopress.

- A work introducing aspects of technology in field archaeology, especially concerning drawings. A valuable update to some reference manuals, e.g. MOLAS.

D'Amore, L. 2014. Stratigraphy in Archaeology: A Brief History, in C. Smith (ed.) *Encyclopedia of Global Archaeology (volume 10/S0)*: 7085–7094. New York: Springer Reference.

- Concise and targeted contributions on archaeological stratigraphy, with additional bibliography.

Stein, G. 2005. The Comparative Archaeology of Colonial Encounters, in G. Stein (ed) *The Archaeology of Colonial Encounters*: 3–32. Santa Fe: SRA Press.

- As with D'Amore 2014 above, concise and targeted contributions on archaeological stratigraphy, with additional bibliography.

Harris, E.C. and R.G. Gunn 1998. The Use of Harris Matrices in Rock Art Research, in P.S.C. Taçon and C. Chippindale (eds) *The Archaeology of Rock Art*: 911–926. Cambridge: Cambridge University Press.

- A general presentation of how Harris matrices can be used to analyse rock art.

Harris, E.C. 1997 (1979). *Principles of Archaeological Stratigraphy*. London: Academic Press.

- This is the manual in which Harris describes his principles of stratigraphy. First published in 1979, and now available in several languages, it is an indispensable complement to this present book for those wishing to go further into the study of stratigraphic matrices. You will find further reading on the history of stratigraphy and specific field methods, well suited to modern archaeology, targeted at producing accurate stratigraphy. Some of the sections dealing with systematic hand drawings and grids are, of course, outdated, but they can easily be translated into modern methods, using photogrammetry and CAD.

Amadori, L., M. Capponi and G. De Rossi 1996. *Esercizi di Matrix*. Roma: Kappa.

- The first book of stratigraphic exercises to appear, featuring valuable case studies, but without explanations; it represents a good complement to this present book, especially in terms of attempts at very hard and extensive exercises.

Browman, D.L. and D.R. Givens 1996. Stratigraphic Excavation: The First 'New Archaeology'. *American Anthropologist* 98.1: 80–95.

- An article dealing with the creation of archaeological stratigraphy and the link between North American and European archaeologists in the 19th and 20th centuries.

Museum of London Archaeology Service 1994. *Archaeological Site Manual.* London: Museum of London.

- Referred to simply as the MOLAS Manual, this is an essential reference work for field archaeologists. Some outdated parts, e.g. on grid matrices and hand drawings, are now updated in works such as Wilkinson 2020, and specific publications about the use of technology in data acquisition, e.g. Kimball 2016.

Harris, E.C., M.R. Brown and G.J. Brown (eds) 1993. *Practices of Archaeological Stratigraphy*. London: Academic Press.

- A good compilation with examples of stratigraphic matrices. Includes representative case studies from around the world.

Online resources

https://leicsfieldworkers.org/resources/fieldwork-guides/

- In collaboration with Leicester University, this site provides very useful documents for archaeologists. Check guide #6 ('A quick guide to archaeological excavation') with its final paragraph about matrices and their main objectives.

http://www.bajr.org/BAJRread/BAJRGuides.asp

- Explore the many BAJR resources for archaeologists. In particular, see page 4 of guide no. 23 ('Record sheet and report templates. Risk assessment forms and other guides') about the stratigraphic matrix.

draw.io

- All the diagrams in this present book were drawn using this freeware.

https://www.youtube.com/watch?v=xv-Yqoktyjg

- An accessible video from *Animated Science* on the Harris matrix (accessed 25.07.2025).

CHAPTER 2.
EXERCISES

Complete the Harris matrix of the following sections and plans.

Exercise 1: Simple succession of layers

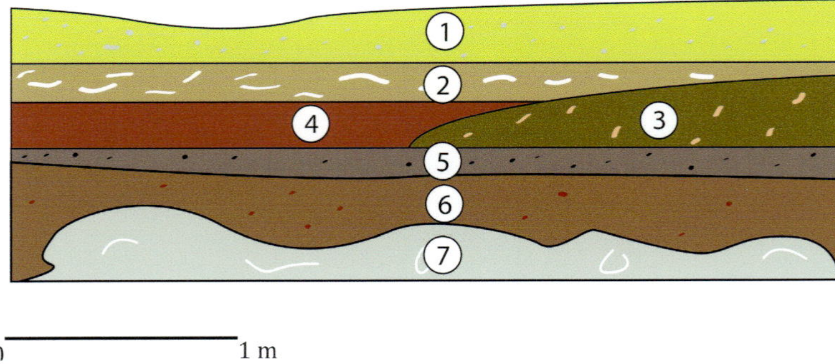

Figure 5: Exercise 1.

Exercise 2: Simple succession of layers 2

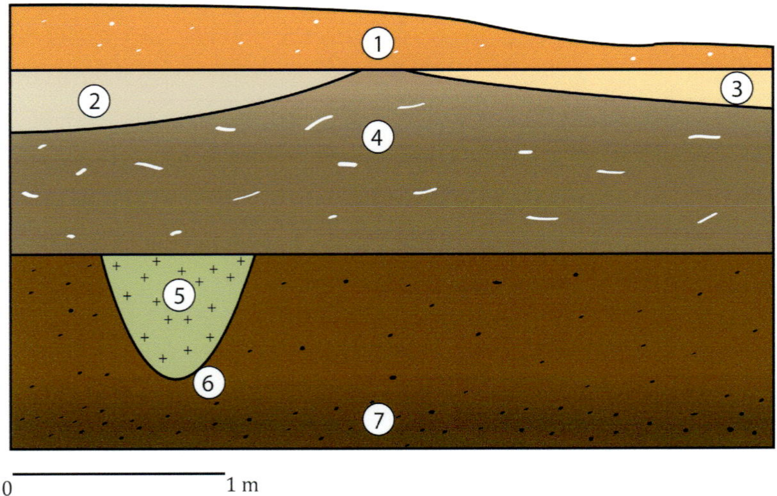

Figure 6: Exercise 2.

Exercise 3: Large pit

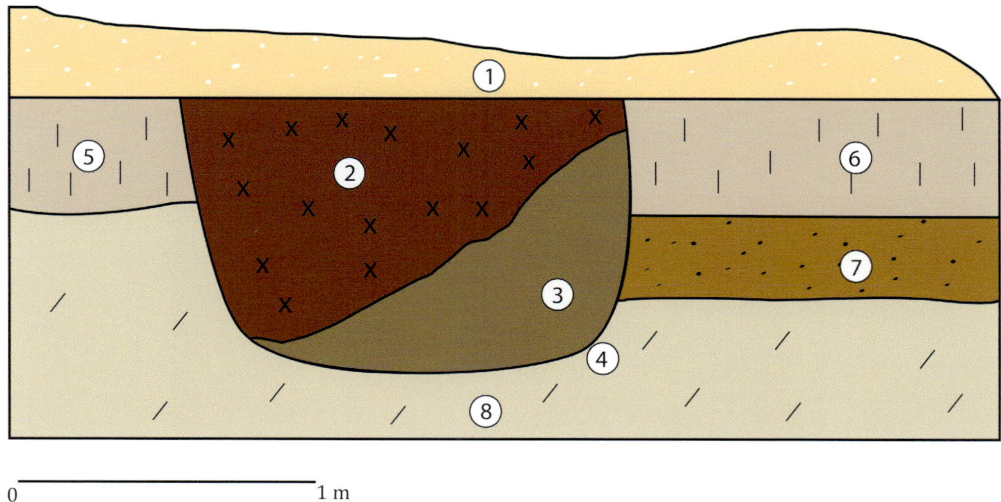

Figure 7: Exercise 3.

Exercise 4: Large pit 2

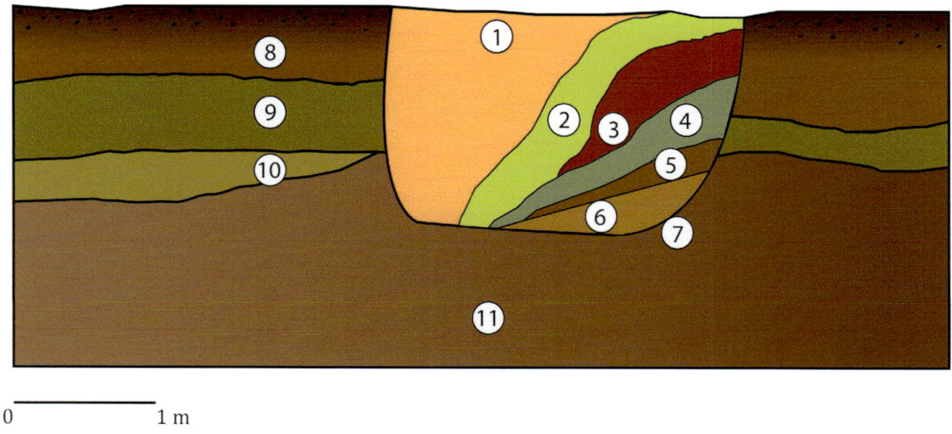

Figure 8: Exercise 4.

Exercise 5: Posthole

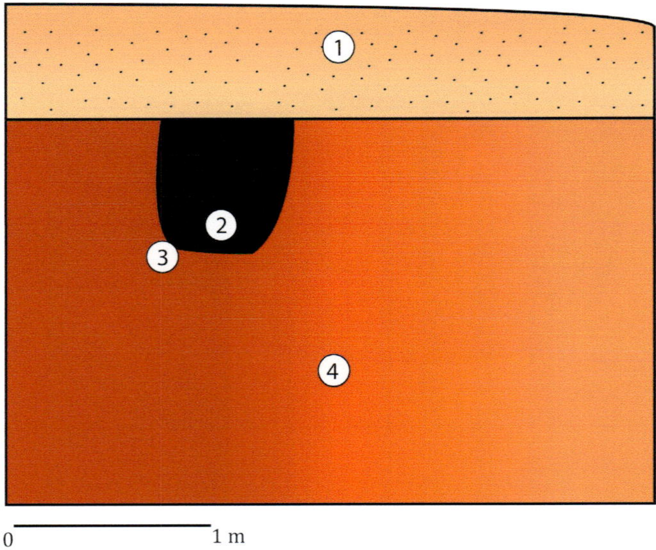

Figure 9: Exercise 5.

Exercise 6: Postholes

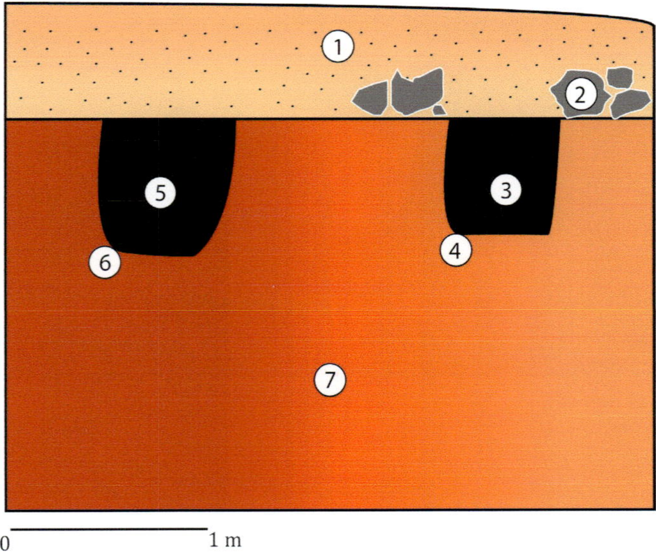

Figure 10: Exercise 6.

Exercise 7: Foundation wall and wall with backfill on one side

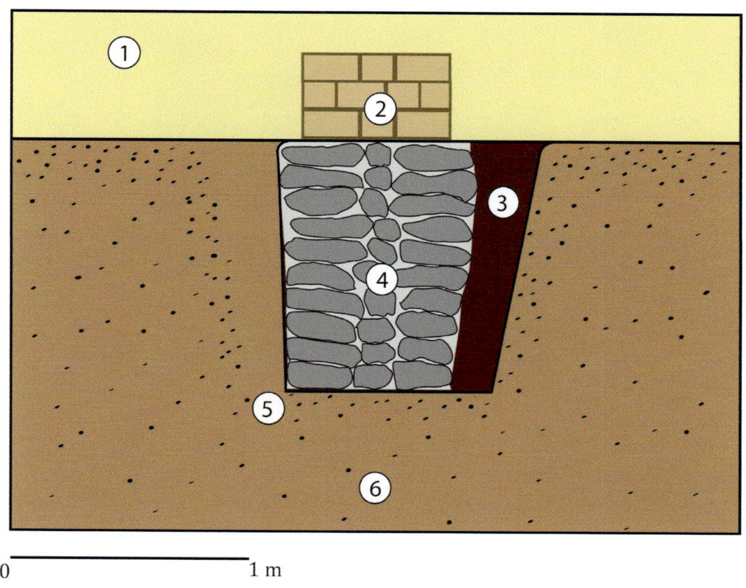

Figure 11: Exercise 7.

Exercise 8: Foundation wall and wall with backfill on either side

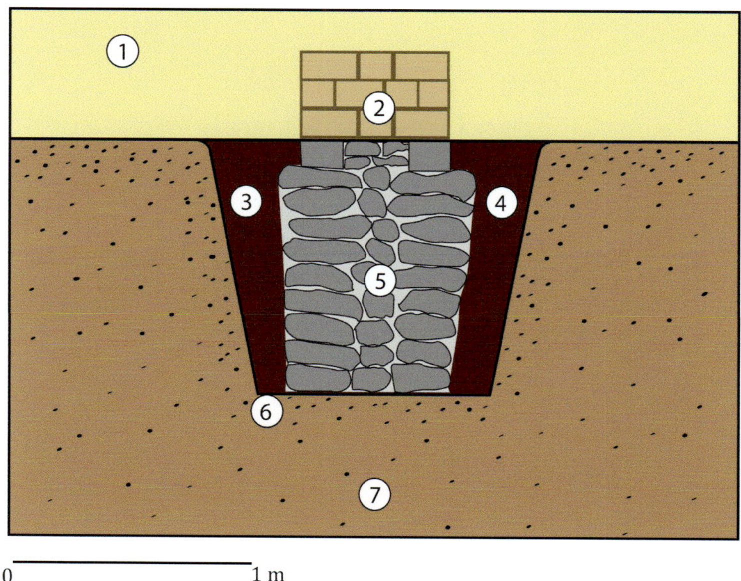

Figure 12: Exercise 8.

Exercise 9: 'Trench build' foundation wall and wall

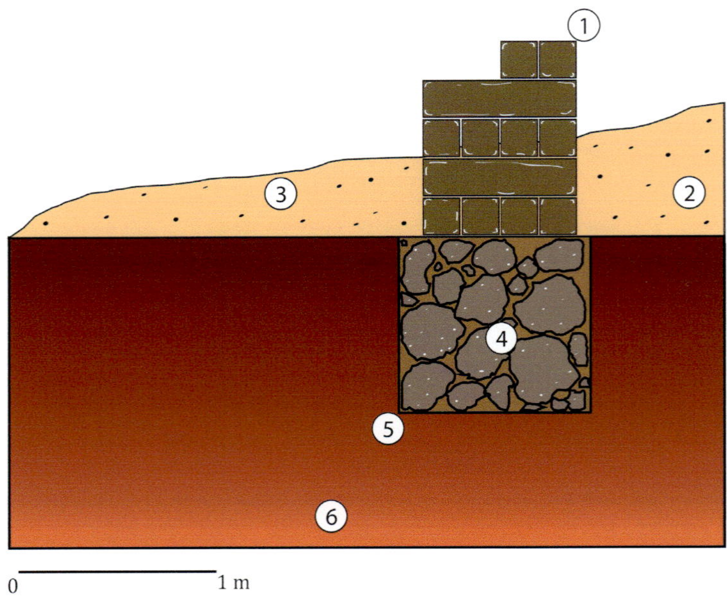

Figure 13: Exercise 9.

Exercise 10: Collapsed wall

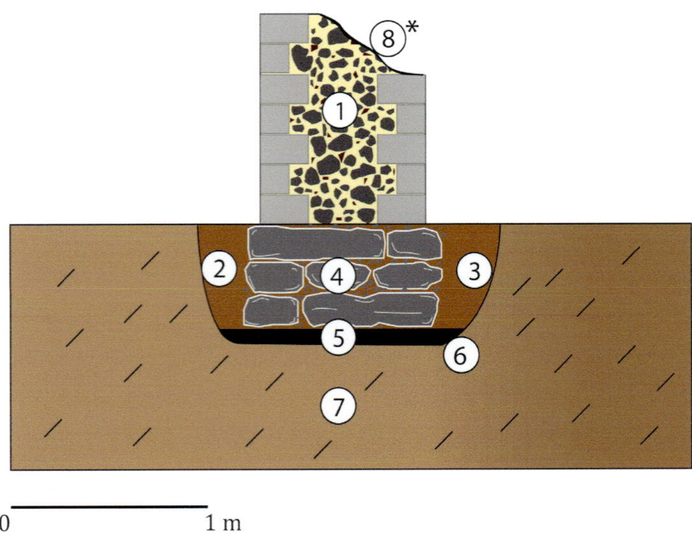

Figure 14: Exercise 10.

Exercise 11: Canalisation

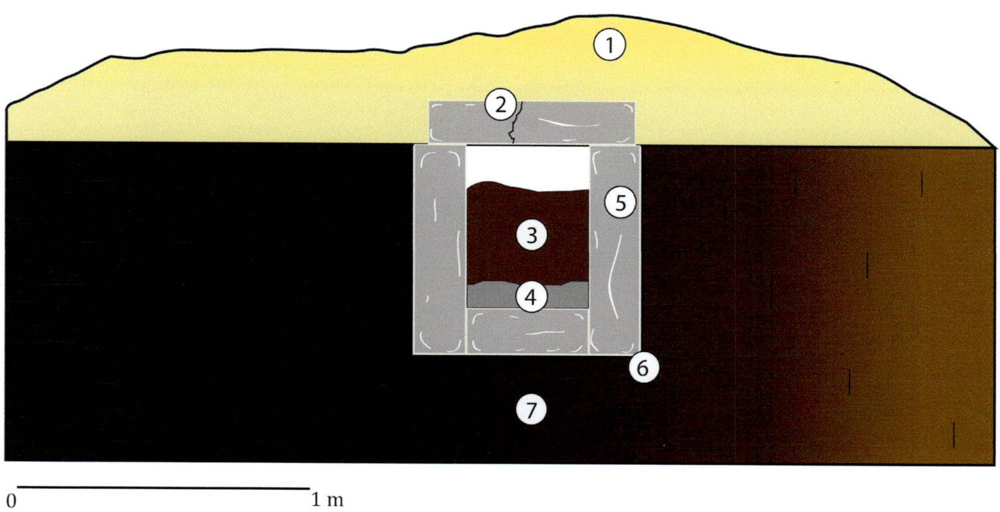

Figure 15: Exercise 11.

Exercise 12: Arabian-style earth architecture

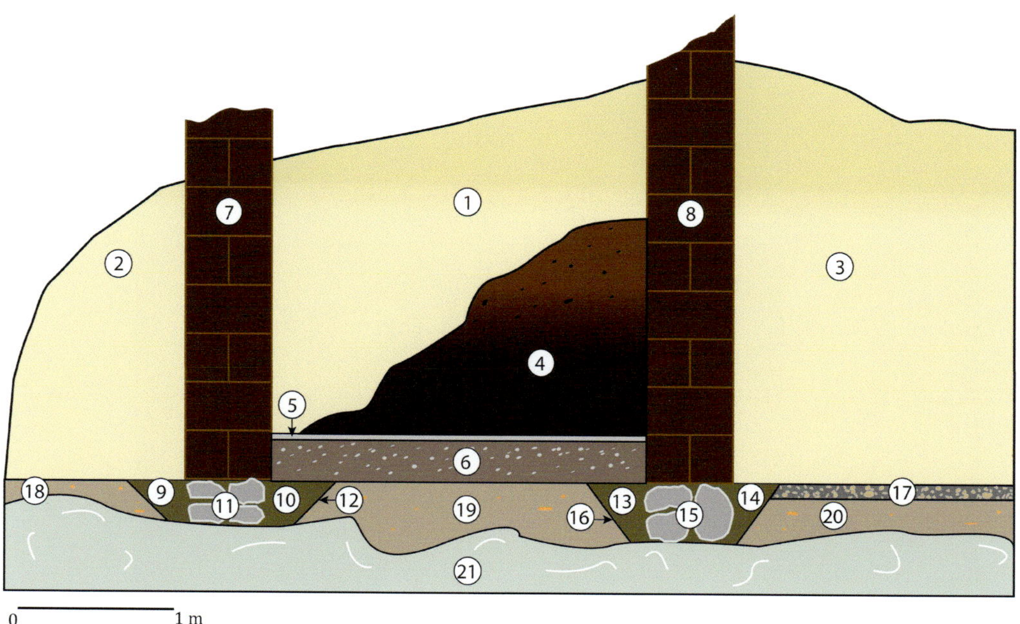

Figure 16: Exercise 12.

Exercise 13: Mesopotamian-style architecture

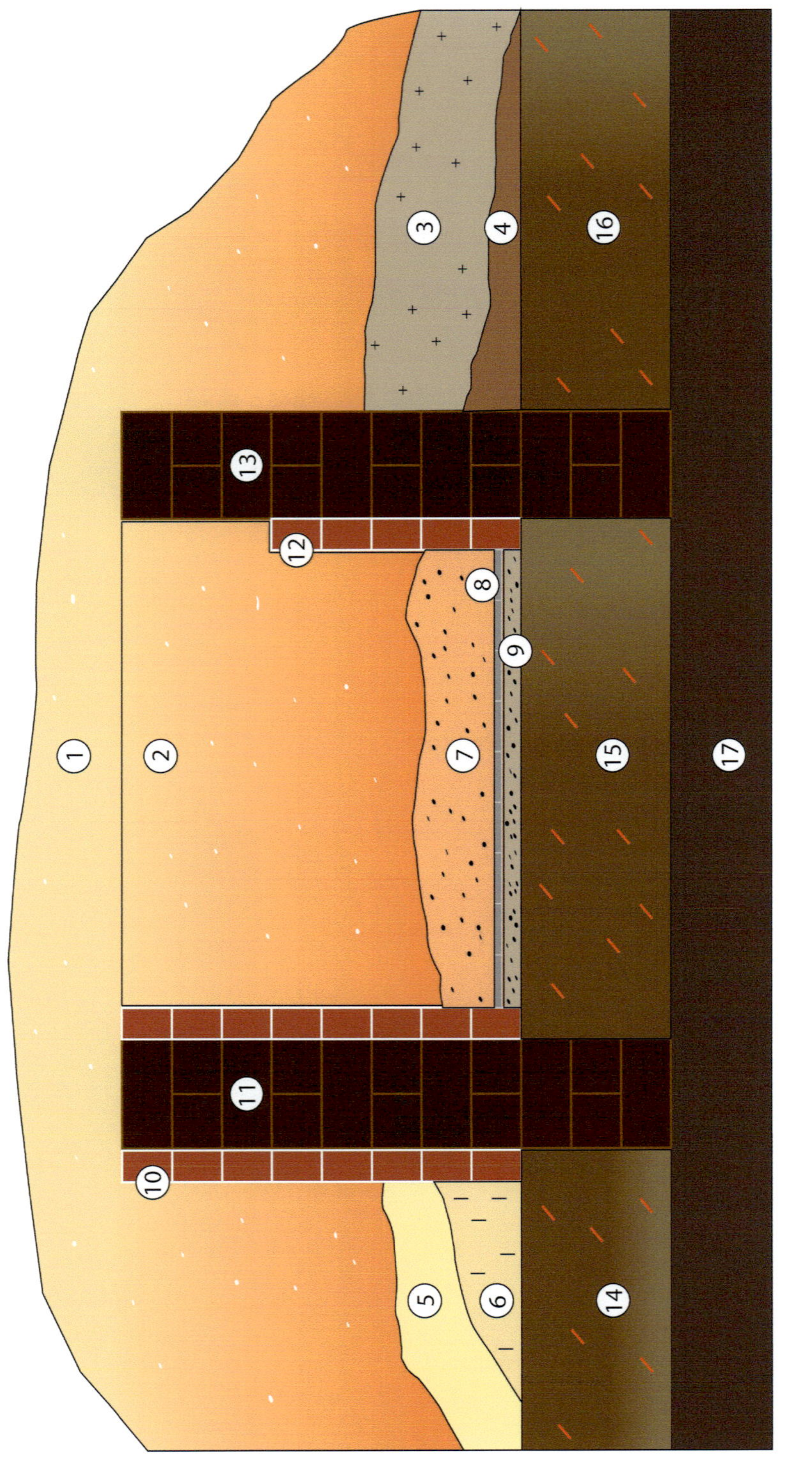

Figure 17: Exercise 13.

Exercise 14: Prehistoric settlement

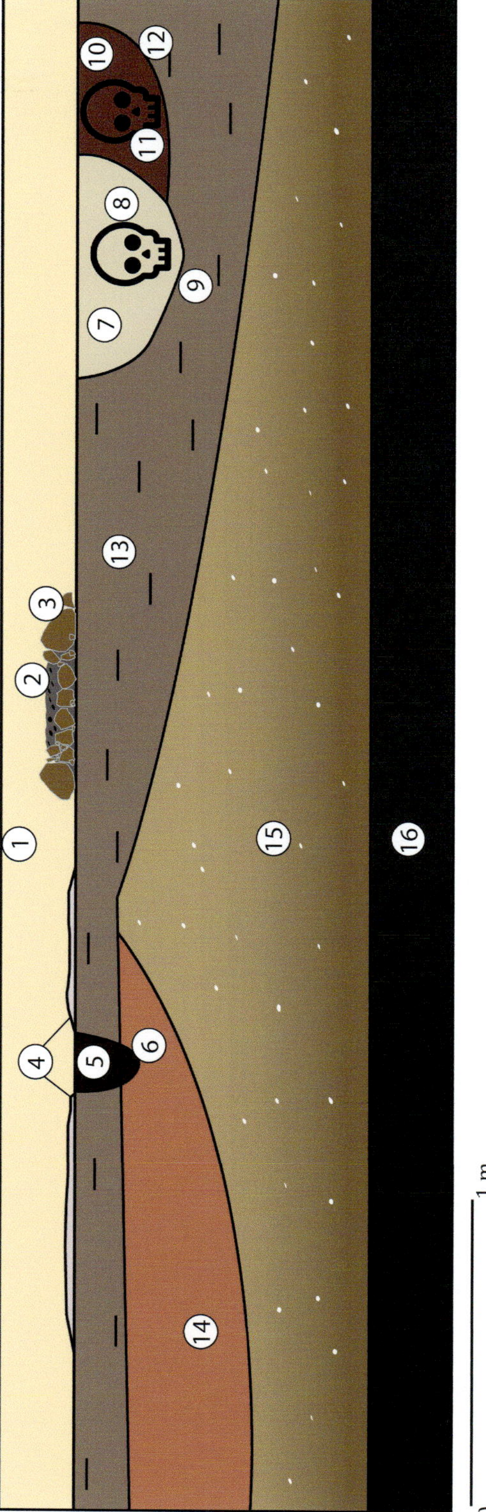

Figure 18: Exercise 14.

Exercise 15: Multi-period site

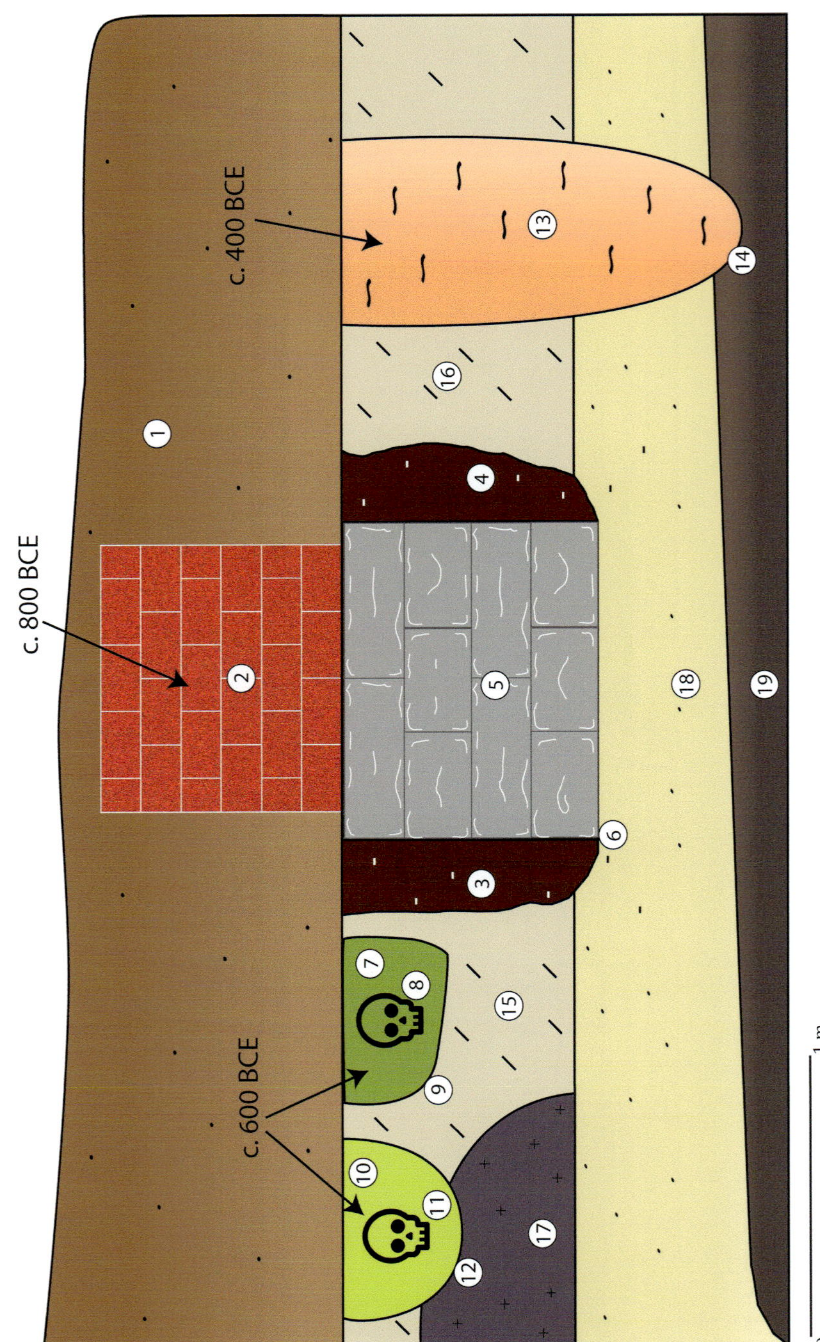

Figure 19: Exercise 15.

Exercise 16: Traditional houses: reuse and conservation

Figure 20: Exercise 16.

Exercise 17: North American pit house

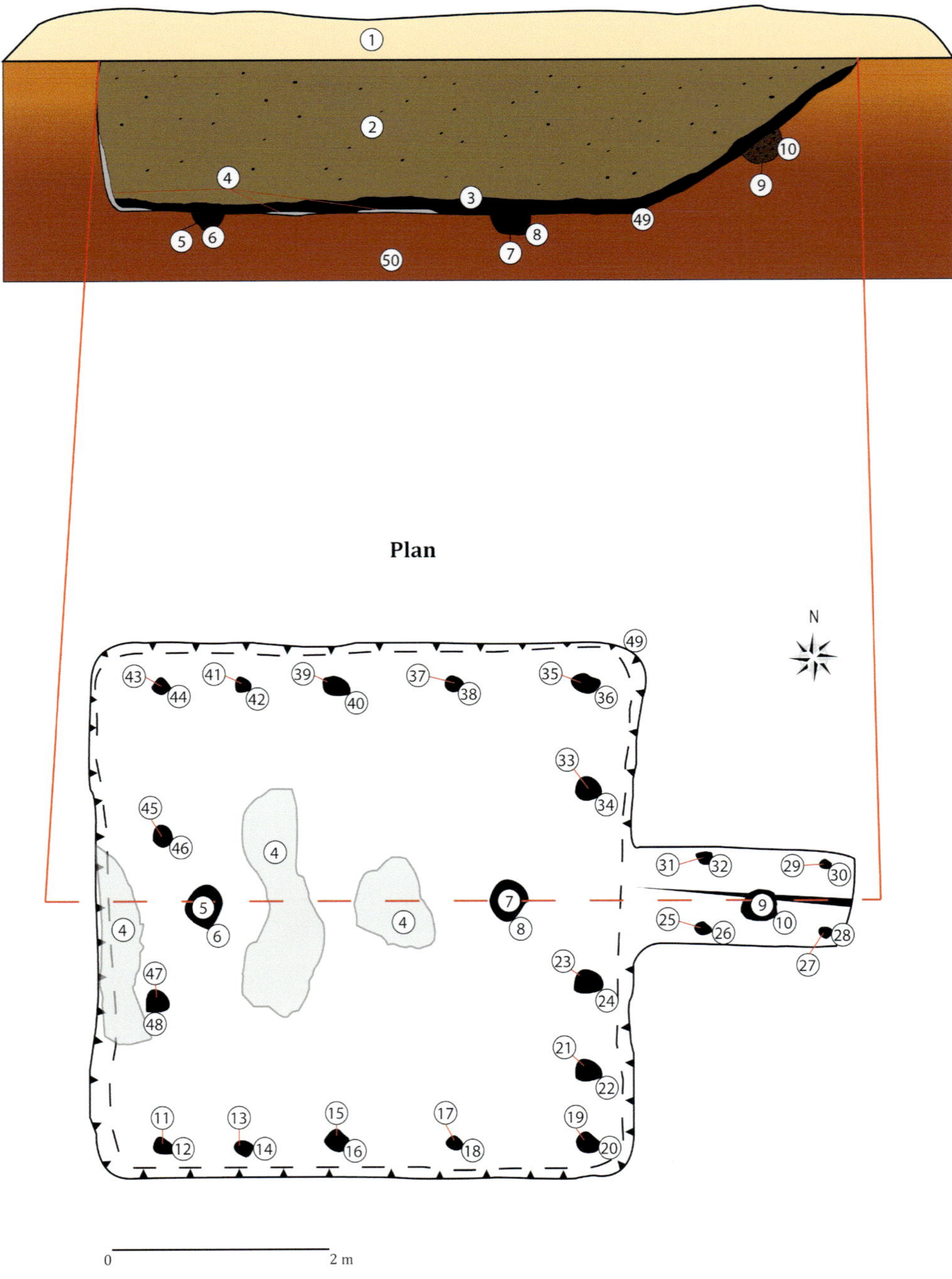

Figure 21: Exercise 17.

Exercise 18: Artisanal area

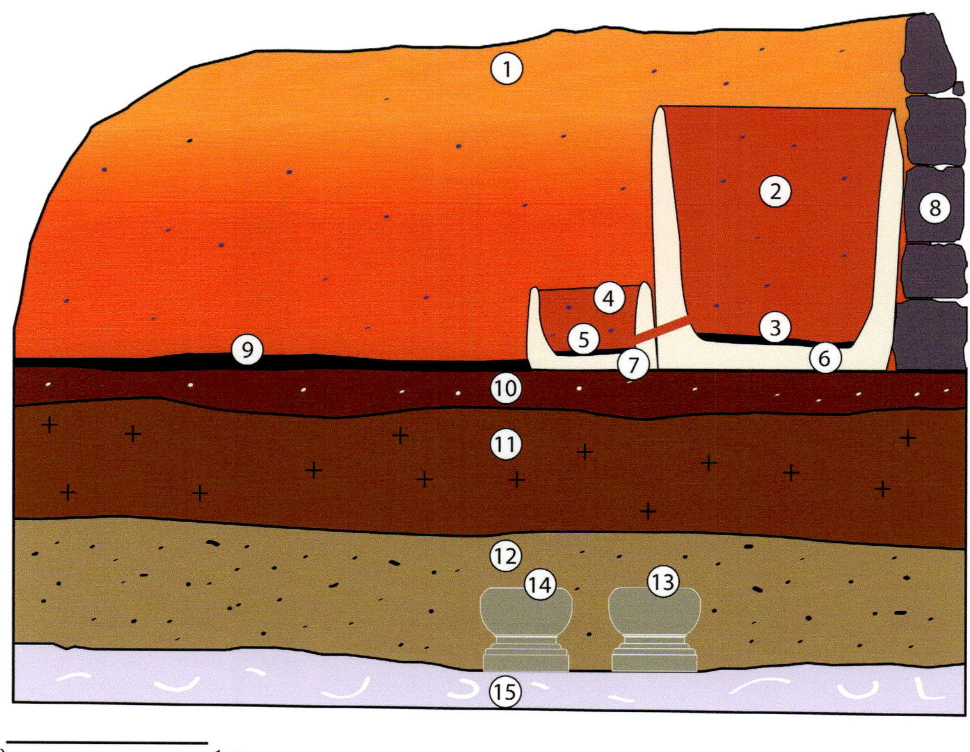

Figure 22: Exercise 18.

Exercise 19: Pottery kiln

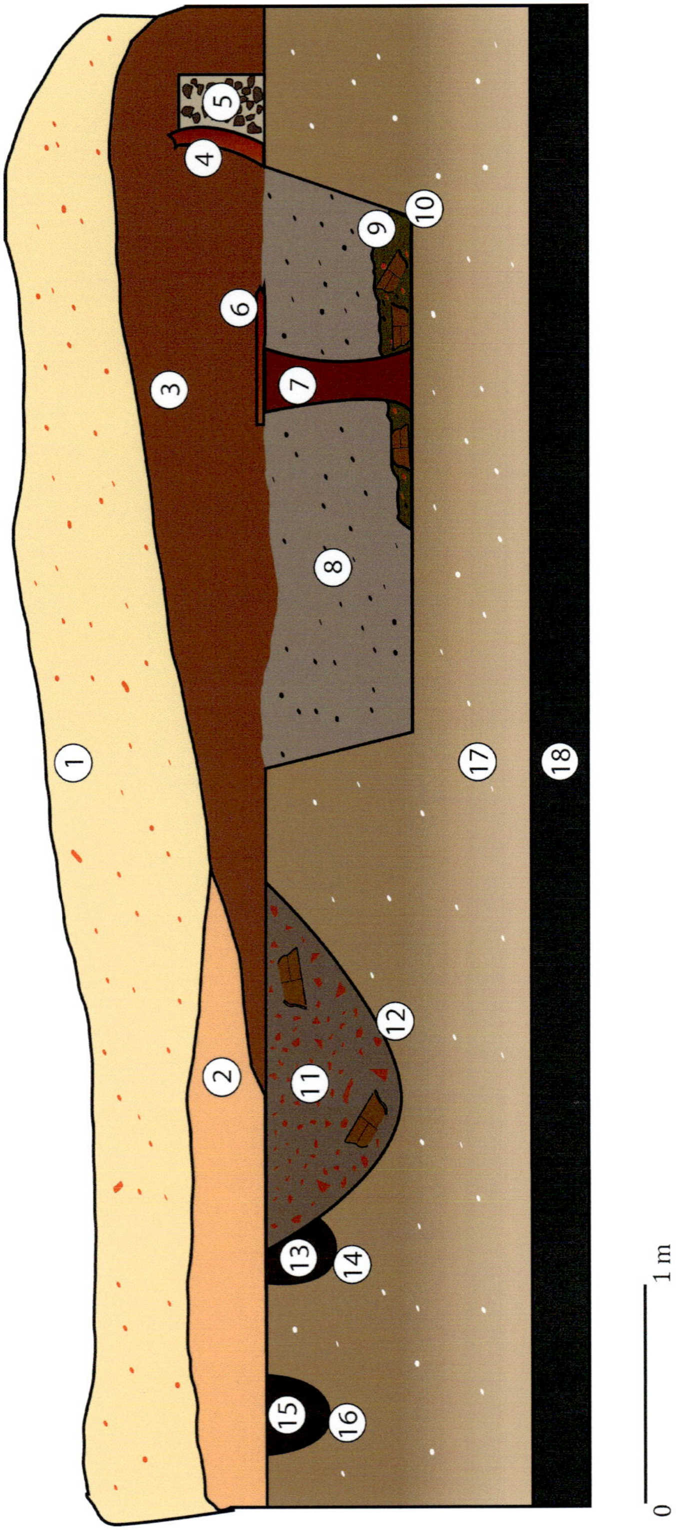

Figure 23: Exercise 19.

Exercise 20: Mediterranean mountainous site

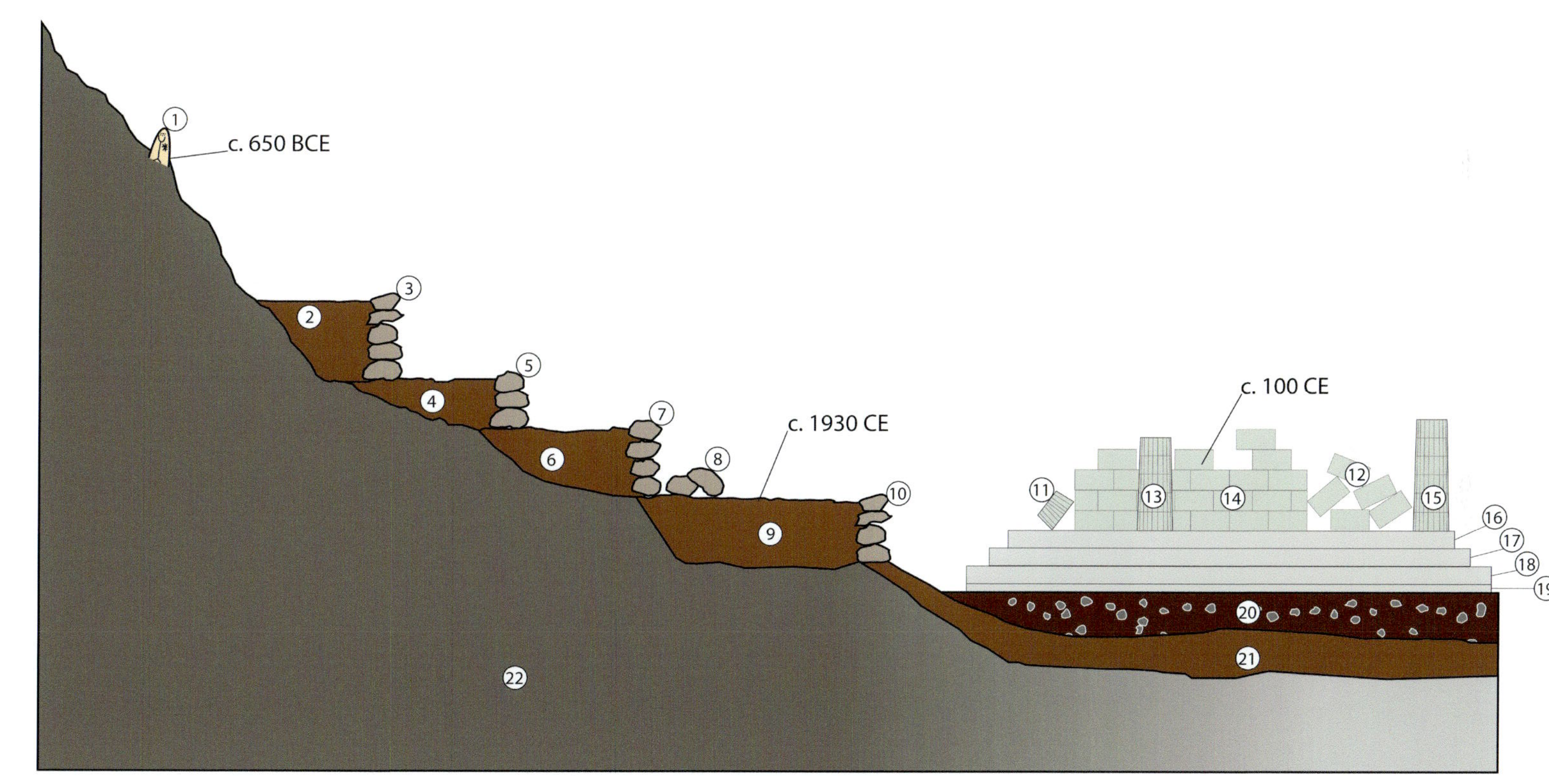

Figure 24: Exercise 20.

Exercise 21: Prior unsupervised interventions at an archaeological site

E-W Section

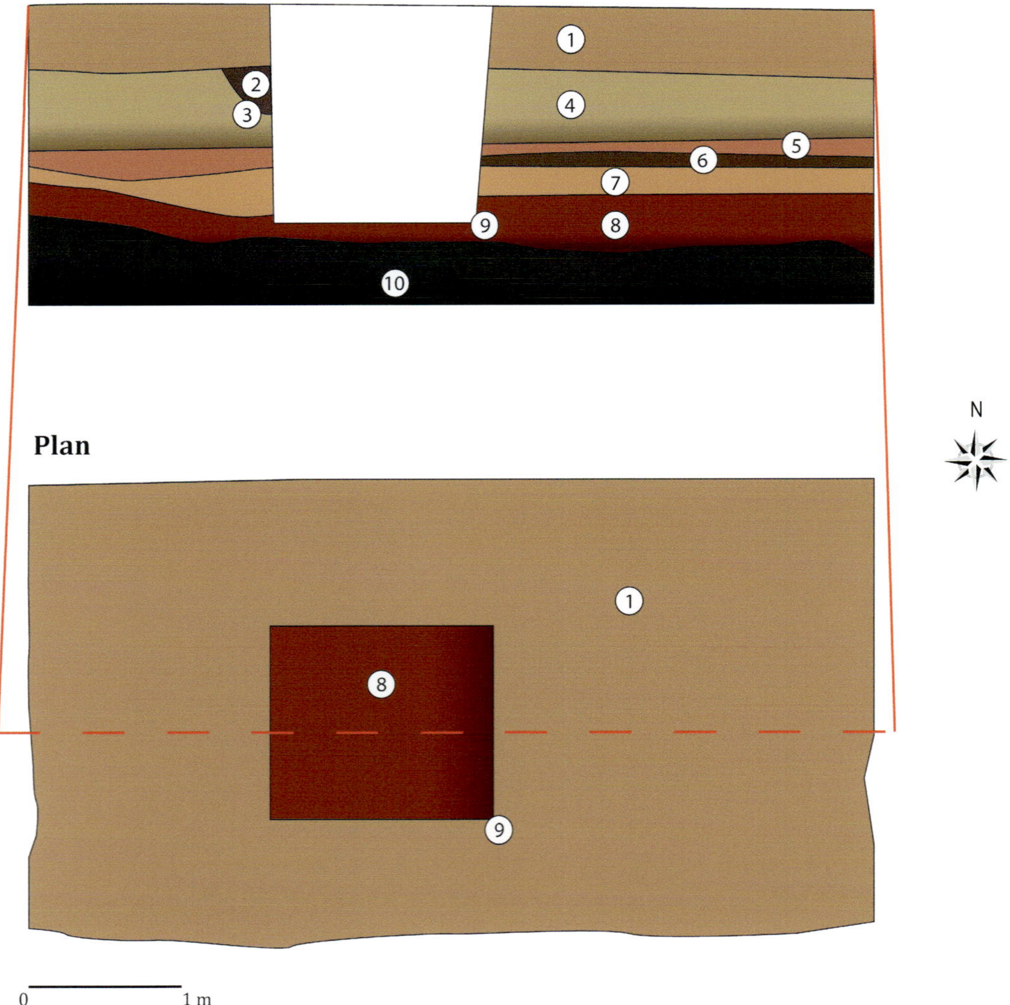

Figure 25: Exercise 21.

Exercise 22: Anglo-Saxon building

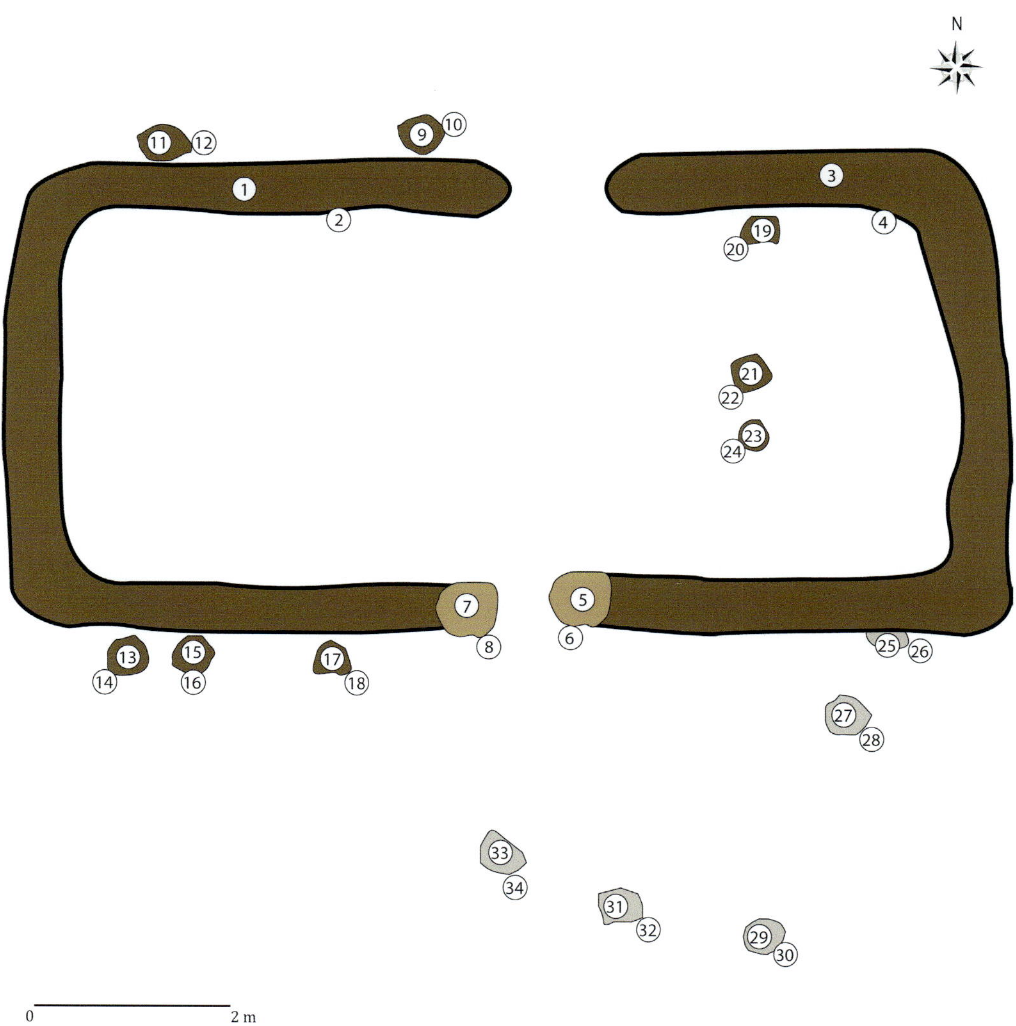

Figure 26: Exercise 22.

Exercise 23: Multi-period rural site

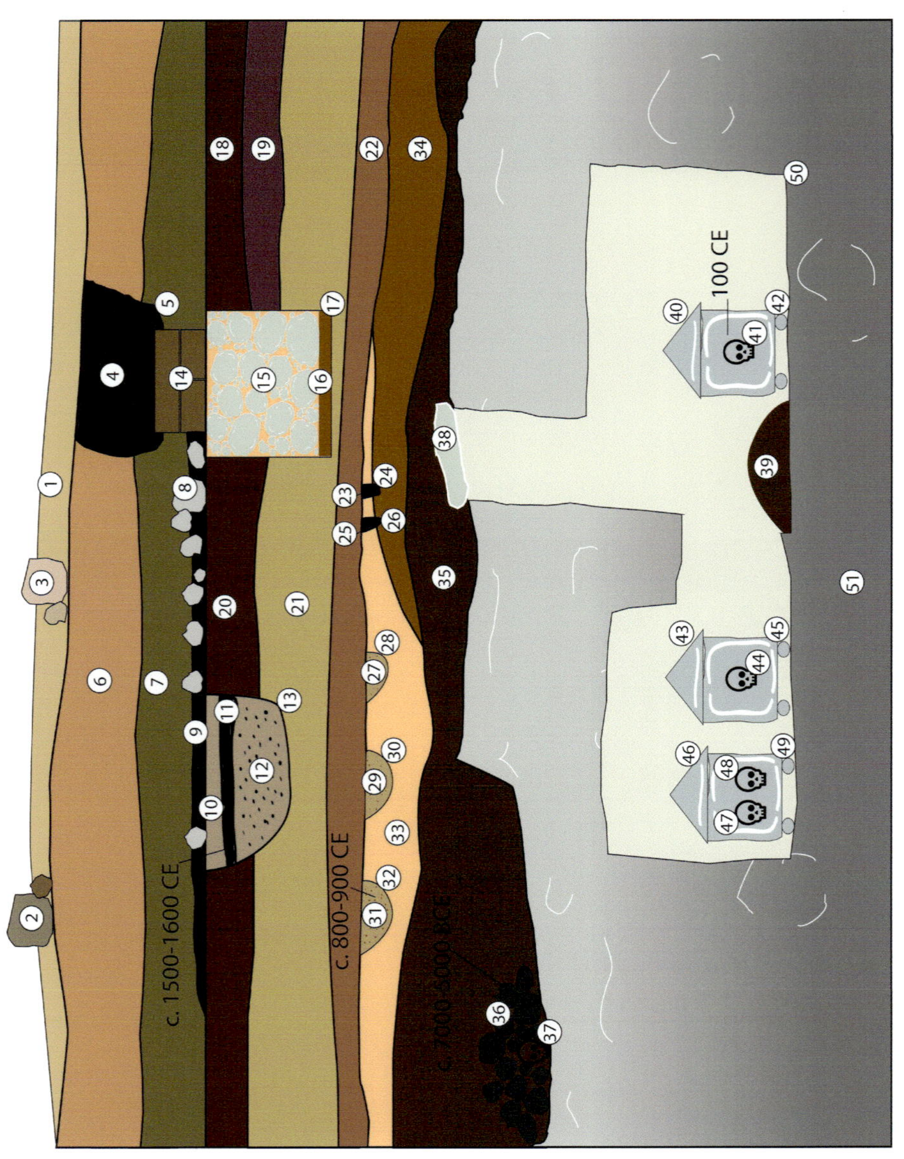

Figure 27: Exercise 23.

Exercise 24: Industrial archaeology

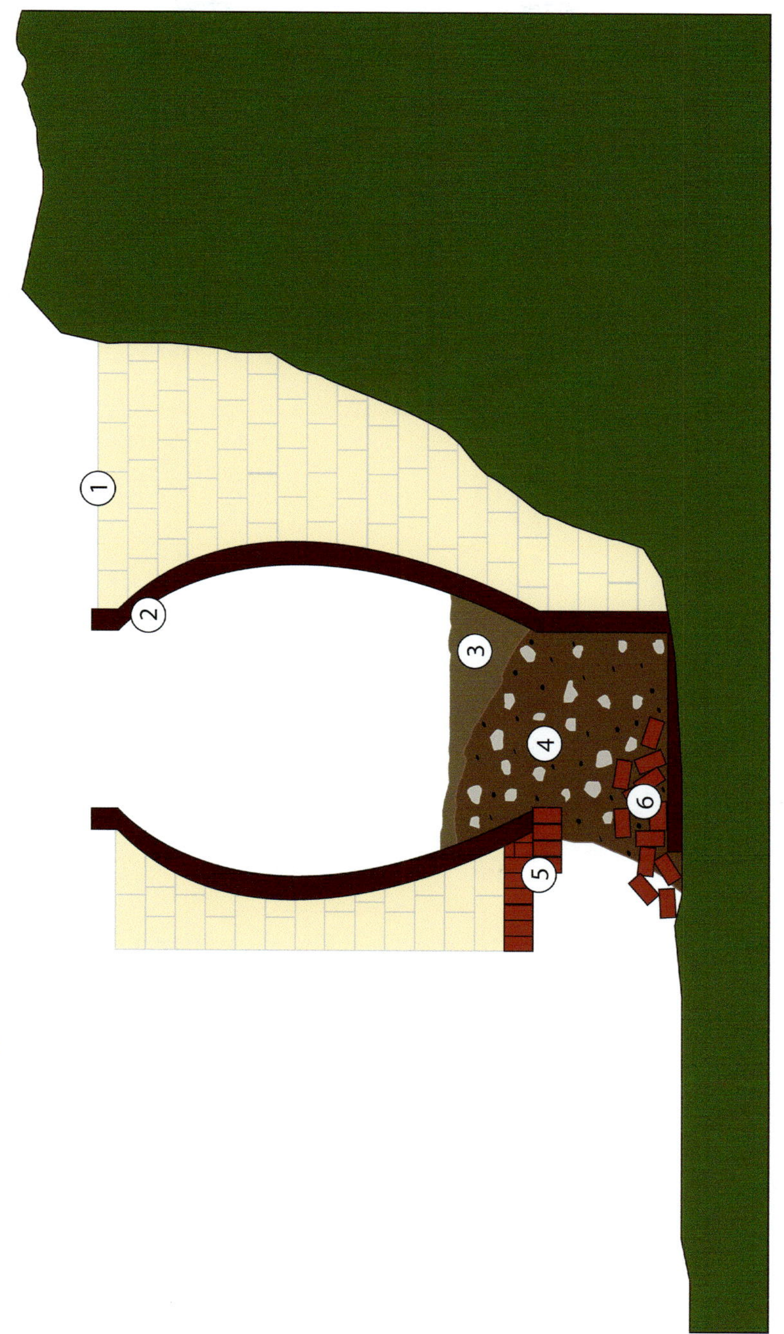

Figure 28: Exercise 24.

Exercise 25: Building archaeology

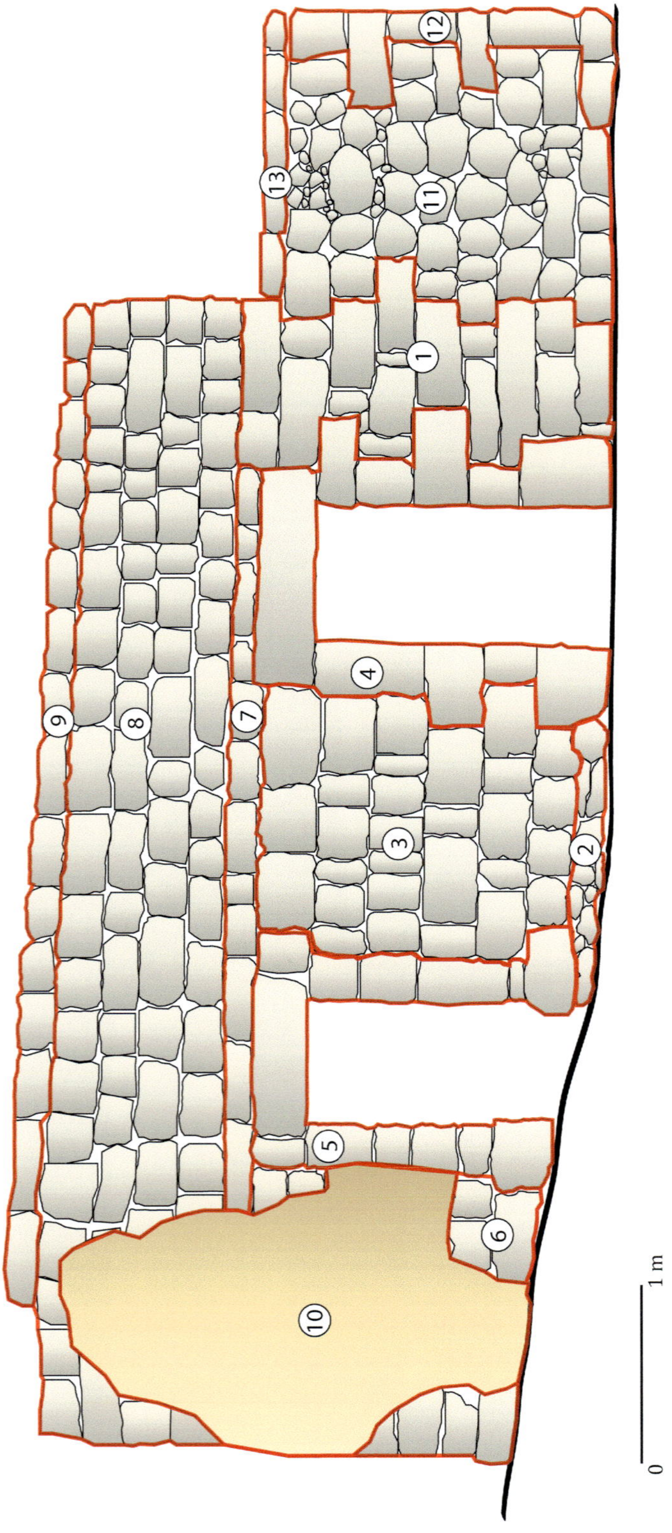

Figure 29: Exercise 25.

CHAPTER 3

EXPLANATIONS AND COMMENTS ON THE EXERCISES

This section provides explanations of the matrices and comments for each exercise.

Exercise 1 (explanation): Simple succession of layers

This exercise presents what we might consider a simple and clear succession of layers (either natural or anthropic) deposited above the bedrock (SU 7).

As in our rule of 'Superposition' above, generally, the higher the deposit the newer it is. But there is an exception to this here: SU 3 is earlier than SU 4, even if it is higher. Here, we know that SU 3 is earlier than SU 4, because SU 4 is above SU 3 – in other words, SU 3 is continuing beneath SU 4. We can also say that all the layers are, or tend to be, horizontal (see 'Original Horizontality'). The matrix shows the clear relation between the deposits, from the latest (SU 1) to the earliest (SU 6), and, finally, to the natural soil (SU 7). Even if SU 2 and SU 3 share an interface, this physical link is not shown by the matrix; the chronological link is a priority here (SU 3 being earlier than both SU 4 and SU 2) – see 'Stratigraphic succession'.

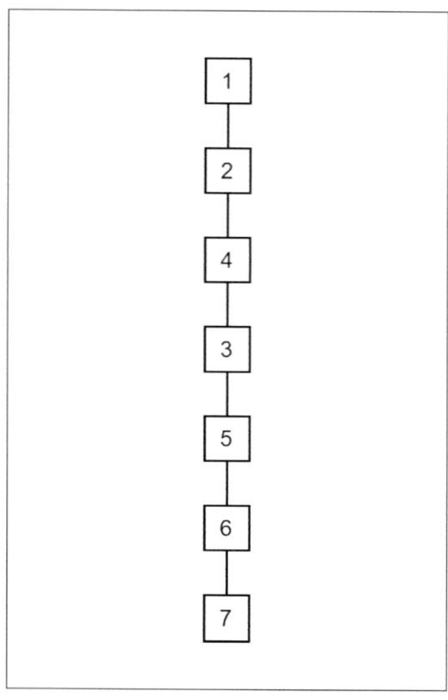

Figure 30: Exercise 1: matrix.

Exercise 2 (explanation): Simple succession of layers 2

This exercise shows an example of accumulated deposits and a pit.

After removing the last accumulation layer (SU 1), the archaeologist has to record two layers (SU 2 and SU 3) deposited above a large layer (SU 4). Without any physical links between the two different layers SU 2 and SU 3, it is not possible to know which of these layers is later than the other; this is why they are at the same level on the matrix. Beneath SU 4, the diggers found a pit – pit cut (SU 6) and pit fill (SU 5) – made inside the natural soil (SU 7). This exercise confirms the rule of 'Superposition', i.e. the higher layers are more recent than the lower ones. Also, it confirms 'Original Horizontality', i.e. all the layers, not being restricted by a narrow basin of deposition, tend to be deposited horizontally. In terms of 'Stratigraphic Succession', the matrix shows

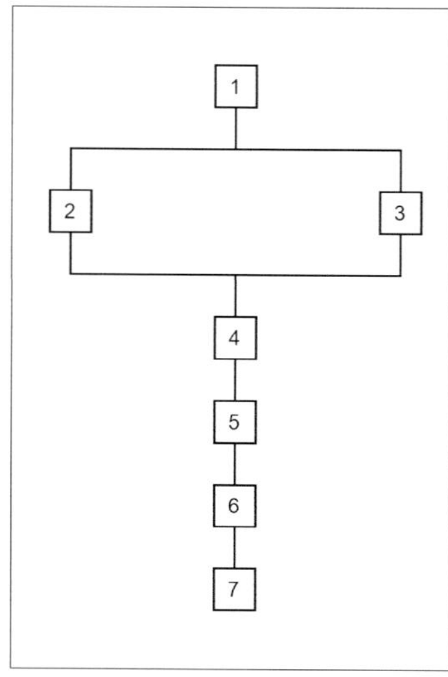

Figure 31: Exercise 2: matrix.

a good example of how superficial relations are deleted. Indeed, even if SU 1 and SU 4 are physically linked, they are not linked in the diagram, as SU 2 and SU 3 are later than SU 4.

Exercise 3 (explanation): Large pit

This exercise shows an example of a large pit filled with two layers.

After removing the last layer of natural accumulation, the archaeologist reaches a large pit. The pit is composed of a cut (SU 4) and two fills – earlier (SU 3) and later (SU 2). The cut was made into levelling SU 5 and SU 6, and natural accumulation layers SU 7 and SU 8. Both the levelling layers and the natural accumulation layers conform to 'Original Horizontality'. The way it was deposited also confirms 'Superposition', the higher deposits being the latest ones. Let's take a look at the relation between the cut (SU 4) and the earlier deposits (SU 5 to SU 8) on the matrix. SU 5 and SU 6 were a single deposit before being truncated by cut SU 4, so, on the matrix, SU 5 and SU 6 have to be joined by a 'same as' link – see 'Original Continuity'. On the matrix, SU 4 is only directly linked with SU 5 and SU 6, even if it is also physically linked with SU 7 and SU 8 on the ground. Only the link that refers to the chronological succession of the events is useful here: SU 4 later than SU 5 - SU 8 (see 'Stratigraphic Succession').

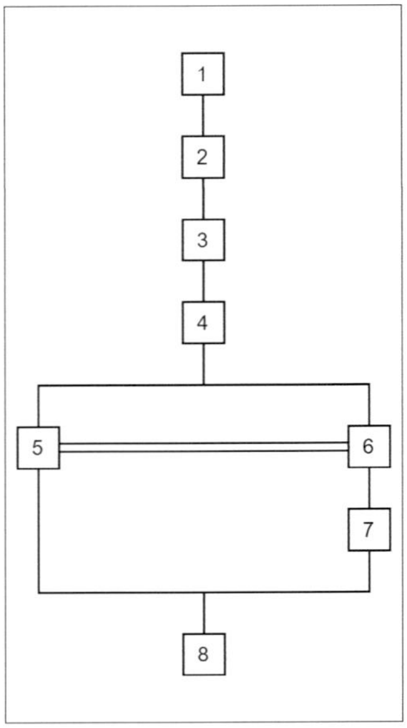

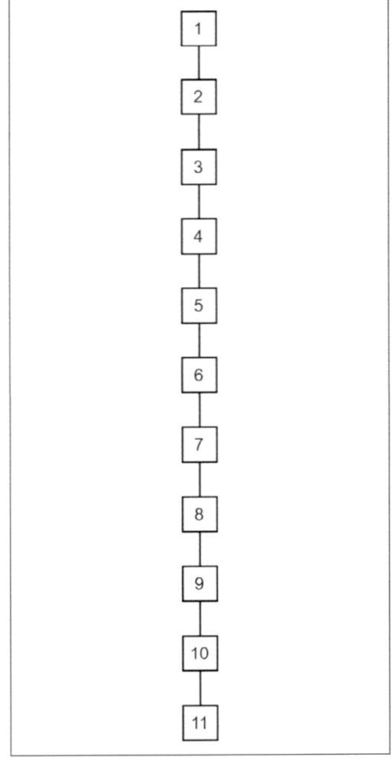

Figure 32: Exercise 3: matrix.

Exercise 4 (explanation): Large pit 2

This exercise shows a large pit with several fills.

The cut of the pit (SU 7) was made in an area where only natural accumulation layers were present (SU 8 - SU 11). The first layers to be recorded are the fills of cut SU 7: SU 1 - SU 6. They are the last events to occur on the site. Cut SU 7 was made into layer SU 8 and cuts SU 9 and SU 11. SU 10 is a natural accumulation layer deposited between SU 11 and SU 9.

This exercise is a good example of what an analysis of the way layers deposited inside a basin of accumulation can reveal. Indeed, it is possible here to notice that the fills of the pit don't follow the rule of 'Original Horizontality': they are accumulated in the right part of the feature. This demonstrates that the deposition process took place from the right to the left part of the feature. These kinds of observations are very helpful to understand the different events behind the formation of the stratigraphy.

Figure 33: Exercise 4: matrix.

Concerning the matrix, it is quite simple, going from the last action (the fills), to the earlier one (the natural soil). Note here that the physical relations between cut SU 7 and SU 9 and SU 11 are not represented – they are not helpful to an understanding of the chronology of the site; only the stratigraphic relations are shown, i.e. SU 7 later than SU 8 (see 'Stratigraphic Succession').

Exercise 5 (explanation): Posthole

Unearthing this posthole, our excavator first encounters the last natural deposition (SU 1), then the fill (SU 2) of the hole dug initially to support a wooden beam. Fill SU 2 is the result of the deterioration of the wood and the filling of the cut (SU 3) with sediment.

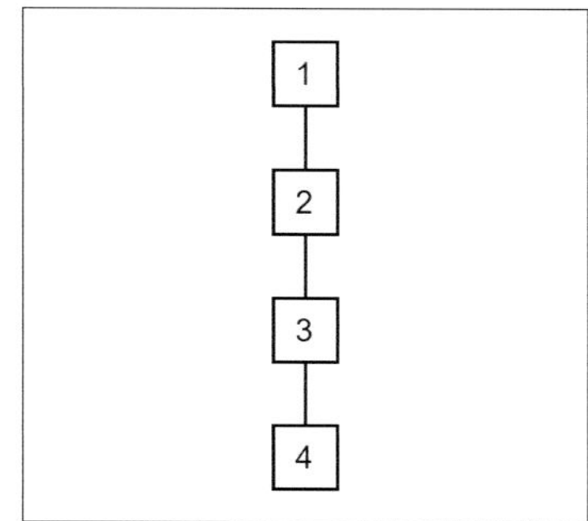

Figure 34: Exercise 5: matrix.

Note that if SU 1 and SU 4 are physically related, they are not directly linked on the matrix by a line. This is because SU 4 – the natural layer already here before the construction of the structure – is the earlier (natural) action of the sequence: thus it is logically at the bottom of the diagram (see 'Stratigraphic Succession'). In other words, SU 1 from one side, and SU 2 and SU 3 on the other, are closer, chronologically speaking, than SU 1 and SU 4.

Exercise 6 (explanation): Postholes

After removing the last natural event (the deposition of sediment represented by SU 1), our archaeologist encounters two postholes, initially dug to support wooden beams as structural elements. The postholes are very similar, except that the right one has preserved its blocking stones (SU 2), initially used to add extra support for the beam. While these blocking elements might seem disparate elements during excavation, especially if just parts are still in situ, they are to be considered as one SU. The introduction of blocking stones takes place, obviously, after the beam has been placed in the hole, explaining why the stones (SU 2) are above any other SU related to the postholes (fills SU 3, SU 5; and cuts SU 4, SU 6).

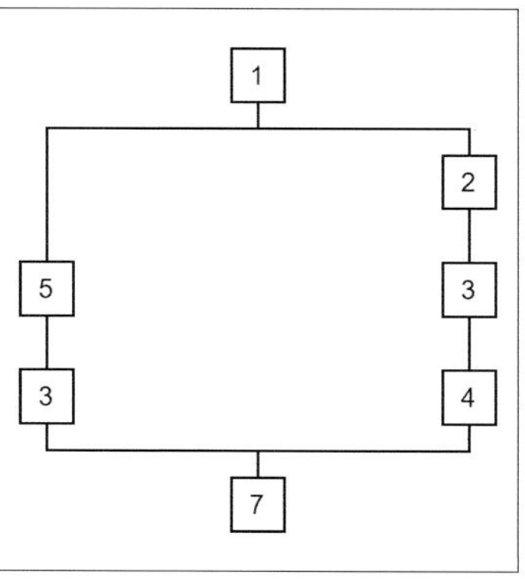

Figure 35: Exercise 6: matrix.

The hole fills (SU 3, SU 5) result from the deterioration of the beams and the filling of the holes/cuts (SU 4, SU 6) with sediment.

Note that even if SU 1 and SU 7 (the natural substratum into which the holes were dug to take the beams) are physically related, they are not directly linked on the matrix. The events leading to supporting the beams (cuts and blocking stones: SU 4, SU 6, SU 2) and those relating to the deterioration of the beams (SU 3, SU 5) are more recent than SU 7 (see 'Stratigraphic

Succession'). Here, we consider that the two postholes are contemporary: identical events (cutting the holes and the deterioration) appear at the same level in the diagram.

Exercise 7 (explanation): Foundation wall and wall with backfill on one side

Exercise 7 shows the remains of a wall and its foundation. After removing SU 1 – a natural deposition layer – we encounter the wall (SU 2), which corresponds to the last action done by the builders. Following the construction from the last event to the first, SU 3, the foundation cut's backfill, is recorded before reaching the foundation wall (SU 4) and the foundation cut (SU 5). Beneath the structure lies the natural (SU 6).

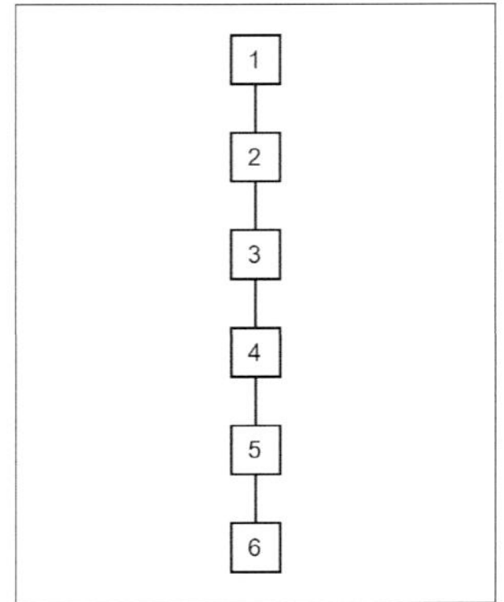

Figure 36: Exercise 7: matrix.

Exercise 8 (explanation): Foundation wall and wall with backfill on two sides

Exercise 8 is very similar to Exercise 7, with the exception that the backfill (SU 3, SU 4) of the foundation cut (SU 6) is from each side of the foundation wall (SU 5). While the two backfills are separate events, our archaeologist must show that they correspond to the same stage of the construction (and that they were probably realised at the same time or over a very short period); thus SU 3 and SU 4 are shown at the same level on the matrix.

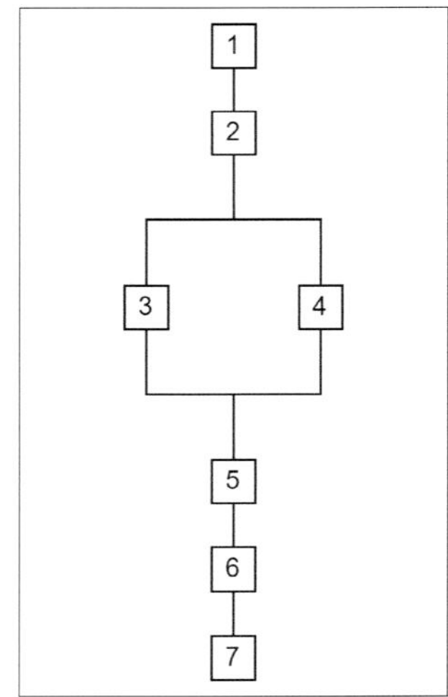

Figure 37: Exercise 8: matrix.

Exercise 9 (explanation): 'Trench build' foundation wall and wall

This exercise involve the remains of a wall (SU 1) and its foundation (i.e. foundation wall SU 4 and foundation cut SU 5) covered by a natural sediment (SU 2, SU 3). The construction of the wall, with its foundation, follows the same process we have already seen in the previous exercises, except that there is no backfill in the foundation cut. This type of foundation cut is generally called 'trench build'.

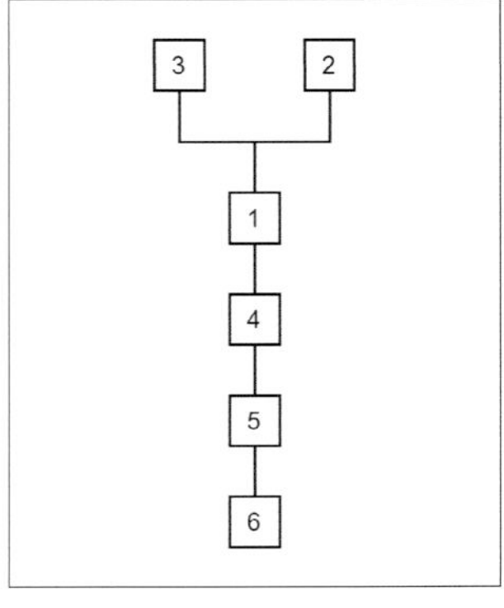

Figure 38: Exercise 9: matrix.

What is interesting here is to note that even if the wall is the higher deposit, it is not at the top of the diagram. Indeed, the natural deposition (SU 2, SU 3), which has not yet had sufficient time to completely cover the structure, is posterior to the wall and logically appears above it on the matrix (see 'Stratigraphic Succession'). Thus, we have here an exception to the rule that higher deposits are more recent than lower ones (see 'Superposition').

Exercise 10 (explanation): Collapsed wall

This exercise deals with the recording of some destruction interfaces as SUs.

Our example is based on a standard wall with its foundation: the superstructure (wall SU 1), the two backfills (SU 2, SU 3), the foundation wall (SU 4), the levelling for the foundation wall (SU 5), and the foundation trench (cut SU 6), followed by the natural sediment (SU 7) into which the wall was constructed.

Notice the collapsed upper part of the wall. A destruction event (natural or not) happened here, and the only clue to this is a part of the upper limit of the wall SU 1 – for many possible reasons, no remains of fallen architecture are found at the foot of the wall. It is possible to stop here, stressing the destruction event occurring to SU 1 in its description. This solution is generally the one most favoured by archaeologists, including myself in many exercises. But, if we follow the rule of '1 action = 1 SU' – even if this SU is not really tangible – it is possible to consider, like Harris does himself, that we need to create an SU to record this destruction, which is an event. Two possible matrices – resulting from two different recording strategies on the ground – can be drawn: one with SU 8 (the destruction of wall SU 1) and one without it.

It is possible to choose either strategy depending on the remains, even if regularity in recording is always preferable, e.g. the remains of damage to a wall that left traces of some specific weapons could be recorded with a specific SU. Thereby, it will be easier and quicker to refer to the traces of the weapons in the report.

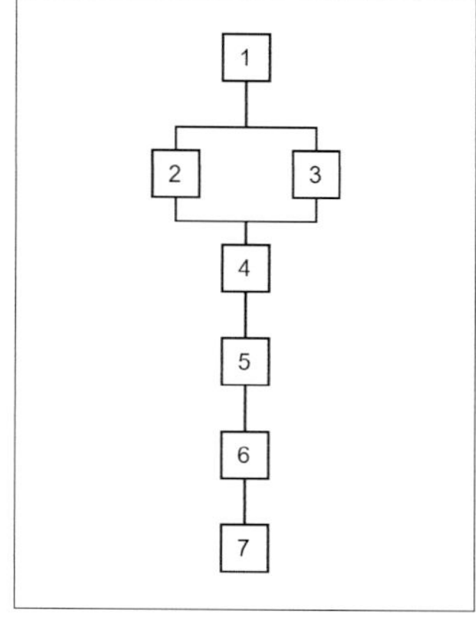

Figure 39: Exercise 10: matrix, version 1.

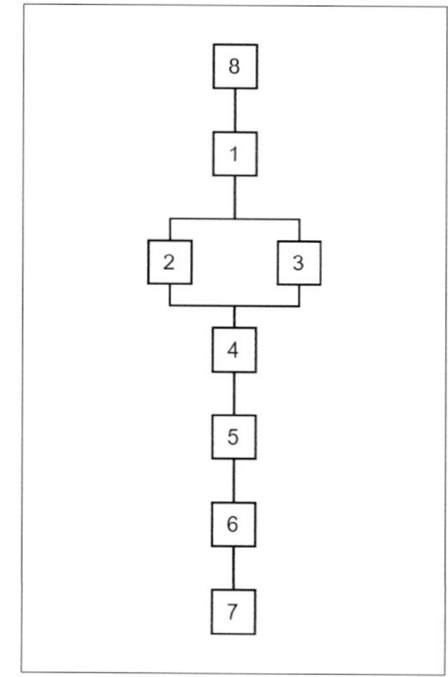

Figure 40: Exercise 10: matrix, version 2.

Exercise 11 (explanation): Canalisation

Exercise 11 shows an example of the digging of a constructed drain in which a natural phenomenon of sedimentation occurred.

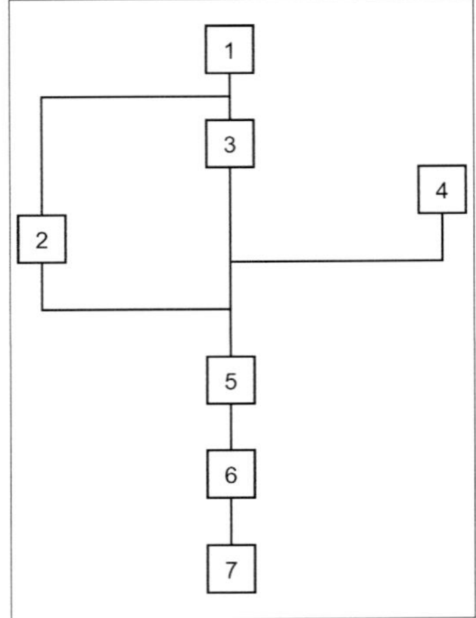

Figure 41: Exercise 11: matrix.

After removing the last layer of natural accumulation (SU 1), our excavator records a drain cover (SU 2). Note that this cover must be recorded singly – even if it is a part of the drain (SU 5) – as it is a movable element. Inside the drain, two layers appear: the later infiltration of sediment (SU 3) and a layer of natural sedimentation (SU 4) resulting from the solidification of the remaining water inside the drain after the abandonment of the structure. Subsequently, the drain (SU 5) and its cut (SU 6) are recorded.

Let's take a look now at the chronology of these events. First, the cut (SU 6) of the drain was made in layer SU 7, then the drain was constructed (SU 5) and covered with slabs (SU 2). After the abandonment of the drain, a phenomenon of sedimentation started (SU 4), followed by infiltration of sediment (SU 3) resulting from cracks that occurred in the cover. SU 1, the natural accumulation layer, is considered here as the last action, even if its process of accumulation could have been partly contemporaneous with the formation of SU 4 and SU 3.

What interests us here is that even though SU 4 and SU 3 are in a lower position, they feature in a later deposit, representing an exception to the 'Deposition' rule. The matrix has to reflect that chronology of deposition by putting SU 4 and SU 3 above the SU linked to the drain (SU 5, SU 2). As the units do not follow each other, in this case it is better to show SU 4 to the side, and not in between SU 3 and SU 5, just to emphasise the special case of later sedimentation inside the structure. SU 2 is placed above SU 5, placed on the side with two physical relationships (SU 1, SU 5) to give a clear view of the events linked to the construction of the drain. It would also have been a possibility to vertically align SU 2 between SU 3 and SU 5.

Exercise 12 (explanation): Arabian-style earth architecture

Exercise 12 shows an example of a mudbrick architecture – used in many places and periods throughout the world. Here, the walls of the house are constructed on small stone foundations placed directly onto the bedrock.

First, our excavator encounters a natural sandy accumulation (SU 1 - SU 3, that fills the space of the remaining building (SU 1) and the space outside it (SU 2, SU 3). Even if SU 1 - SU 3 are due to the same natural event – the natural accumulation of sand – they have not been grouped into one SU because they are separated by walls SU 7 and SU 8 on the ground. Notice also that while walls SU 7 and SU 8 are the highest structures to be recorded, they are not the latest; this is the natural accumulation SU 1 - SU 3, even if it did not have time to cover all the structures. This is an exception to our rule of 'Superposition'.

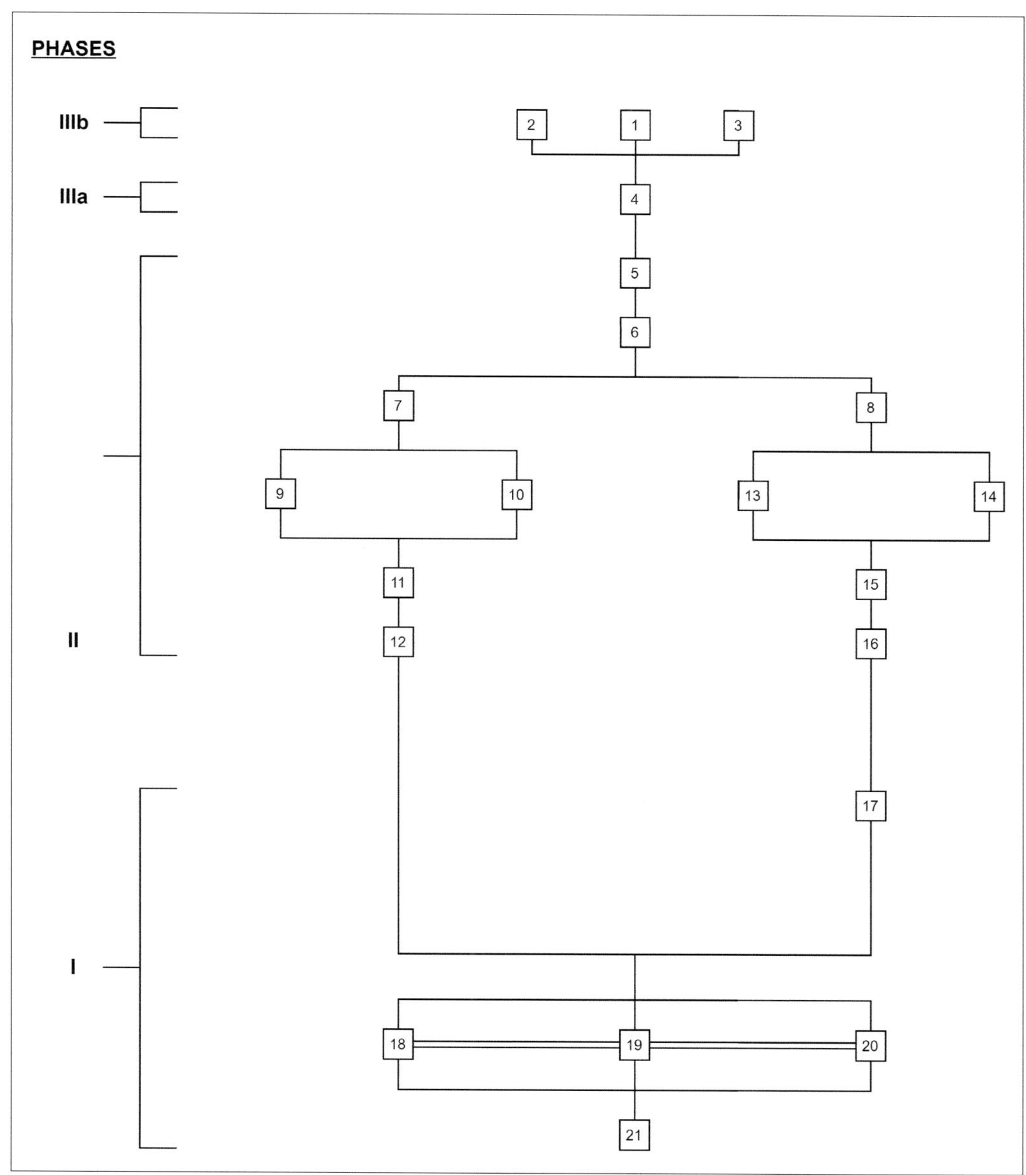

Figure 42: Exercise 12: matrix.

Three SUs inside the building were recorded: SU 4, a collapsed layer, probably from wall SU 8; SU 5, a lime plastered floor; and SU 6, a preparation layer for floor SU 5.

After the layers inside the house, the two walls and their associated SUs are recorded. On one side we have wall SU 7 (with its foundation (backfills SU 9 and SU 10, foundation wall SU 11, and foundation cut SU 12), and, on the other side, wall SU 8 (with its foundation backfills SU 13 and SU 14, foundation wall SU 15, and foundation cut SU 16). The two foundation cuts

(SU 12, SU 16) are cut into an earlier, single layer now divided into three SU (SU 18 - SU 20). This layer was a levelling for an old floor, of which only a small part (SU 17) was conserved to the right of wall SU 8.

SU 17 is not associated with any architecture, and it is cut by the late foundation cut SU 16. On the matrix, SU 18 - SU 20 are linked with a double line, meaning they were a single level before being cut by the two foundation trenches SU 12 and SU 16 (see 'Original Continuity').

After the removal of SU 18 - SU 20, our archaeologist reaches the bedrock. Notice that the two cuts SU 12 and SU 16 have no real bottoms – their bottoms are actually interfaces between the bedrock SU 21 and layers SU 09 - SU 10 and SU 13 – SU 14.

Now, let's look at the translation into phases of all these SUs. On the bedrock, during the earlier phase of the area's occupation, the inhabitants levelled the ground (SU 18 - SU 20) to build, probably, some masonry unit or small features. From these 'constructions', only a small part of a pebbly floor is still visible (SU 17). This corresponds to Phase 1. During Phase 2, others came and constructed the house characterised by the two walls SU 7 and SU 8. From our data it is clearly difficult to say what happened to the superstructure of the first phase of occupation, but it seems that everything was cleared before the construction of Phase 2. The builders dug into the earlier floor and levelling of Phase I to reach the bedrock and build on it the foundation of the walls. For some reason, at the end of Phase two the house partially collapsed and was abandoned. After the abandonment, a natural aeolian accumulation of sand was deposited across the entire area. For more accuracy, our investigator's decision was to subdivide Phase III into IIIa (collapse) and IIIb (natural accumulation).

Exercise 13 (explanation): Mesopotamian-style architecture

This example shows a particular way of building up a wall and its foundation used in ancient Mesopotamia. The technique (called *tamlu* by the ancient Assyrians) involves erecting a single mudbrick wall and then burying the lower part of it, with this part now acting as a foundation.

After removing a first, large, natural accumulation layer (SU 1), our archaeologist has to record the accumulation inside the building (SU 2). Even if the accumulation inside (SU 2) is the same as the large one outside (SU 1), we have to make a clear distinction between them in the recorded data; as such, any material from the accumulation inside the building will be linked to the building itself *only*, and not to the spaces both inside and outside the building. After achieving this, the successive deposits outside the building (SU 3 - SU 6), and a layer (SU 7) deposited directly above the floor of the building have to be removed.

The whole superstructure of the building is now revealed: i.e. the paved floor (SU 8) and its preparation layer (SU 9), and the two walls (SU 11, SU 13) made with sun-dried mudbrick and their facing of fired bricks (SU 10, SU 12). After the identification of these SUs, it is the time to record the man-made deposits (SU 14 - SU 16) used to bury the lower part of the walls. Even if this is represented by a single event, it is preferable not to record them with a single SU number as they are not interconnected.

Here, the question of making a 'same as' link between SU 14 - SU 16 might be raised, but it will depend on whether we want to employ a stricter or looser understanding of the term. The strict definition is that 'same as' implies the connecting stratigraphically of two layers that were physically linked in the past, but were separated by later events; whereas a looser definition is that the term is used for identical layers resulting from the same single event. Our strict definition, which is probably the better one, will not let us to make a 'same as' link between SU 14 - SU 16. If, however, we were to choose the looser meaning, it could lead to the consideration of identical and contemporaneous events as 'same as' (i.e. the backfills of foundation trenches), which might not be helpful in terms of providing a general, quick and clear reading of any matrix. This is why we won't add a 'same as' link here for SU 14 - SU 16. Nevertheless, our archaeologist needs to be aware of both possibilities, with their advantages and disadvantages.

At the end of our excavations, we reach layer SU 17, the natural, on which the initial walls of the building were erected.

The matrix shows the different phases of construction – which are particular here. First, the walls are erected on the natural (SU 17), before being partially buried by SU 14 - SU 16. At this stage, the builders added the facings of fired bricks (SU 10, SU 12) and constructed the roofing (which is not conserved here) and the floor (SU 9, SU 8). The relationship between the deposits that occurred after the abandonment, and especially between the three groups (1 = SU 4, SU 3; 2 = SU 6, SU 5; 3 = SU 7) that followed, cannot be understood for certain as they are not interconnected. We have decided here to put on the same level the first (SU 6, SU 4) and second (SU 5, SU 3) deposits outside the buildings, and to put the deposit (SU 7) found inside the building in the middle. All these arrangements are purely hypothetical.

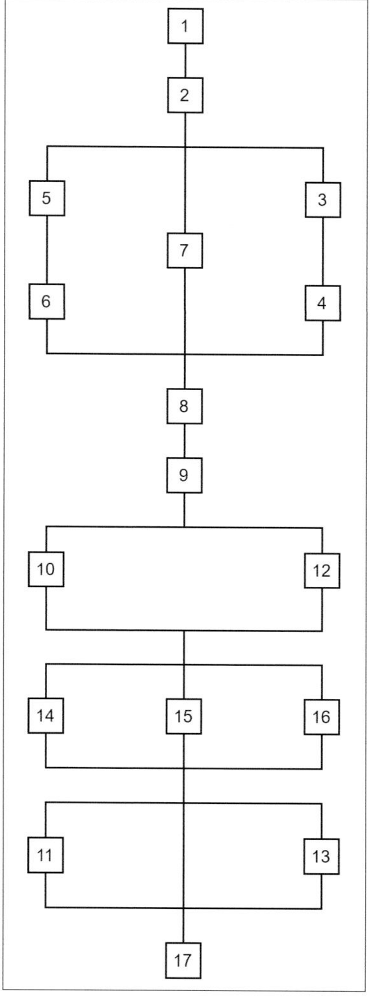

Figure 43: Exercise 13: matrix.

Exercise 14 (explanation): Prehistoric settlement

This exercise shows an example of a prehistoric installation. The first deposit to be recorded is SU 1, the natural accumulation layer. Notice that it is horizontal, like many layers that slowly accumulated over time and were not restricted by any kind of basin (see 'Original Horizontality'). After SU 1, our archaeologist finds the remains of prehistoric occupation, characterised, first, by a small housing unit, i.e. floor remains SU 4 and a posthole (made up of SU 6, the cut originally designed to support a wooden beam, and SU 5, the later fill of the hole after the deterioration of the wooden beam; secondly, by a hearth (SU 3) with combustion remains inside (SU 2); and, thirdly, two graves (SU 7 - SU 9 and SU 10 - SU 12).

This little housing unit was probably a small circular building, with wooden roofing held by a central beam, and a plastered floor. The hearth was associated with the house in an outside space used for several household activities, e.g. cooking. The two graves, cut directly into the earth, are represented (from later to earlier events) by a burial cut (SU 9, SU 12), skeletal remains (SU 8, SU 11), and a burial fill (SU 7, SU 10). These burials are most probably linked to the same occupation phase as the house and its hearth. We note that one of the graves cuts the other, i.e. burial SU 9 cuts burial cut SU 12 and burial fill SU 10, meaning that the burial represented by SU 7 - SU 9 is later than burial SU 10 – SU 12. Posthole SU 6 was cut into deposits SU 13 and SU 14.

The matrix only shows the relationship between SU 6 and SU 13 – the physical link between SU 6 and SU 14 being superfluous (see 'Stratigraphic Succession'). The matrix has to show the chronology between the two burials, explaining why they are represented one above the other on the matrix. In this case, while the two burials are cut into SU 13, the only useful stratigraphic link is the one showing the chronology, and not the physical connection; thus there is no link between the cut of the later burial SU 9 and layer SU 13 (see 'Stratigraphic Succession'). SU 15, the last deposit before the natural (SU 16) is physically linked to SU 13 and SU 14. On the matrix, the only meaningful chronological link is the one showing the succession from the later to the earlier deposit: SU 13, SU 14, SU 15, and SU 16 (again, see 'Stratigraphic Succession').

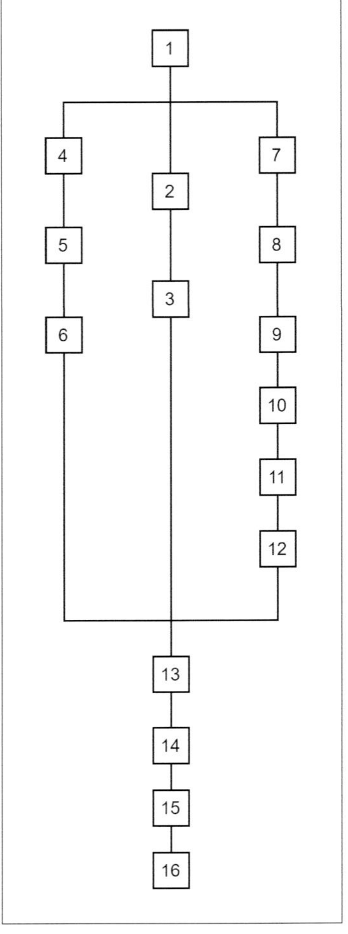

Figure 44: Exercise 14: matrix.

Exercise 15 (explanation): Multi-period site

Exercise 15 explores a multi-phase area. The matrix represents the phasing (i.e. the grouping of SUs by phases) according to the dating of the material and the stratigraphic succession.

After removing the first layer (SU 1), the features appear, i.e. a wall and its foundation (SU 2 - SU 6); two earthen graves (SU 7 - SU 9 and SU 10 - SU 12; and a pit and its fill (SU 14, SU 13). Only later analyses of the finds allowed our archaeologist here to determine the chronology between these features.

The wall is similar to what we found in Exercise 8. It comprised (from later to earlier events) a wall (SU 2), two backfills (SU 3, SU 4), taken as part of the same construction phase, a foundation wall (SU 5), and a foundation cut (SU 6). The foundation cut was made into earlier

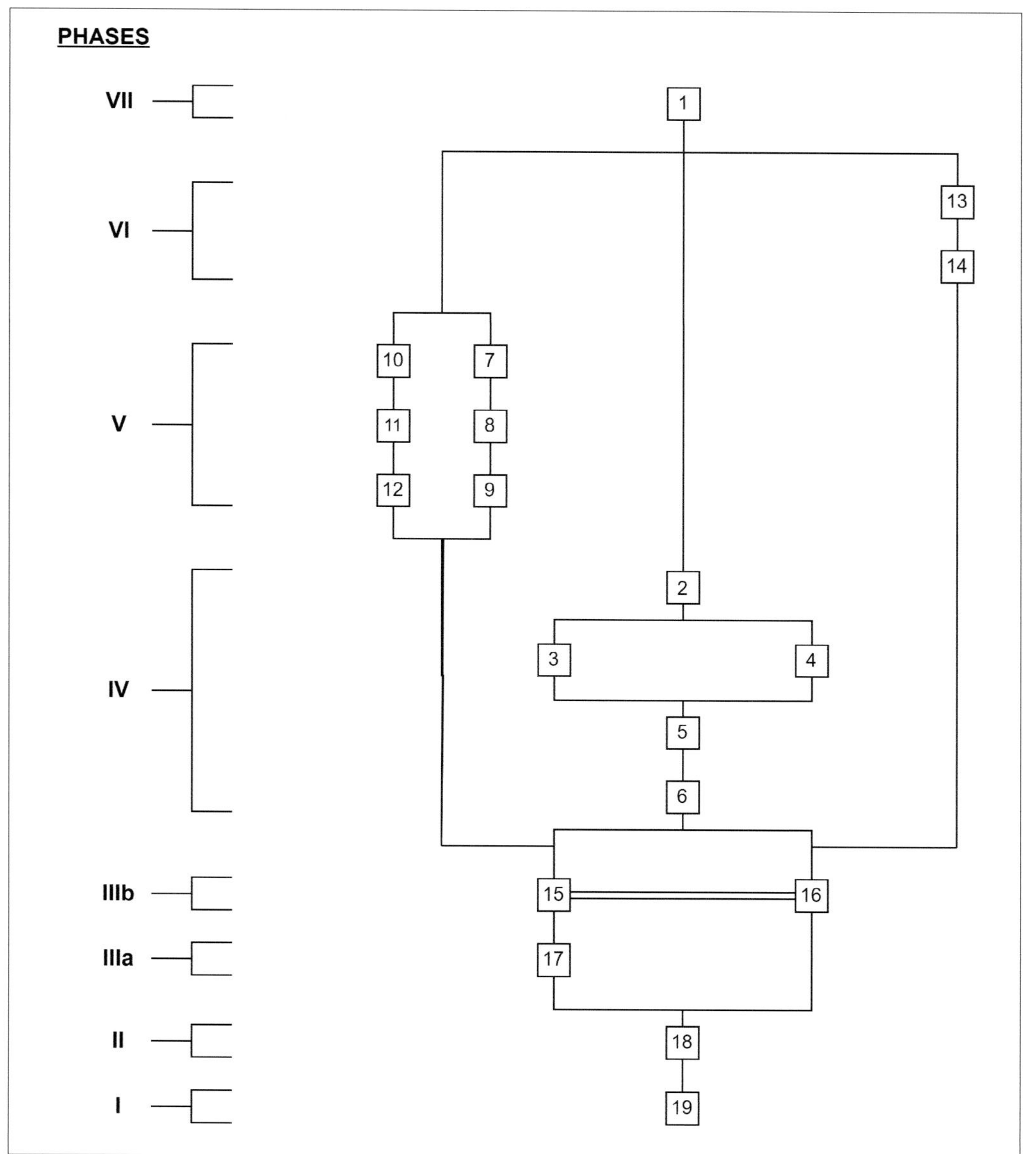

Figure 45: Exercise 15: matrix.

layers (SU 15, SU 16, SU 18). As SU 15 and SU 16 were the same layer before being separated by the construction of the foundation cut, our archaeologist has to identify that relationship on the matrix by linking them with a double line (see 'Original Continuity'). Layer 17 was also present before the construction of the foundation cut and the formation of the layers corresponding to SU 15 and 16; as it has no physical relationship with SU 16, it is showed only under SU 15. Layers SU 15 - SU 17 can be tentatively interpreted as dumps used for levelling purposes.

The two graves have the same characteristics, consisting of a fill (SU 10, SU 7), introduced after the deceased had been placed in the cut, a skeleton (SU 11, SU 8), and a cut (SU 12, SU 9) made directly into the earth. The left grave was cut into two layers: SU 15 and SU 17. The physical relationship between SU 12 and SU 17 is superfluous, thus it is not shown on the matrix (see 'Stratigraphic Succession'); it has no bearing on our understanding of the chronological links between the layers.

The pit is a deep cut (SU 14) cutting into three layers (SU 16, SU 18, SU 19). It has one fill (SU 13). As we have just seen in terms of the relationship between SU 12 and SU 17, the only useful link to be marked on the matrix between the cut of the pit (SU 14) and the other layers is the one between SU 14 and SU 16, which neatly shows the chronology between all the relevant deposits.

The SUs corresponding to the three features we have just reviewed are grouped according to their chronology. The highest are those corresponding to the pit, which, with a dating to *c.* 400 BCE, is the newer construction. It is followed by the two graves, dated to *c.* 600 BCE, and, eventually, the wall and its foundation, the oldest constructions unearthed (*c.* 800 BCE). All these features, along with other layer depositions, are grouped by the following phases.

Phase VII is the latest, corresponding to the natural deposition after the area was abandoned. The pit corresponds to Phase VI. The two graves, while they are contemporary, are grouped under Phase V. Phase IV is confined to the construction of the wall. Phase III, subdivided into IIIb and IIIa, represents SU 15 - SU 17. Here, we should also consider placing Phases IV and III (or at least IIIb) in the same phase if we want to hypothesise that the levelling of Phase III is to be associated with the construction of the wall. But, in the absence of any strong clue, it is better to stay on the safe side. Phases II and I correspond respectively to natural deposition and the topsoil.

Exercise 16 (explanation): Traditional houses: reuse and conservation

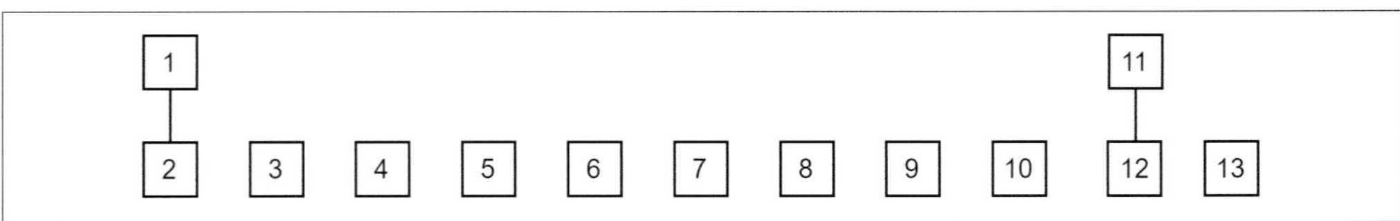

Figure 46: Exercise 16: matrix.

As well as routine emergency archaeological work, professional archaeologists might well spend much of their time in close cooperation with conservation architects on projects involved with the reuse or protection of sites. 'Traditional' houses recorded as 'heritage' represent perhaps one of the most common examples around the world of where archaeologists and conservation architects collaborate. Generally, the archaeologist has to 'clear' a structure and reach the last dwelling floor before architects start their conservation work. The buildings might well then be conserved for various functions, e.g. tourism, or put to some other purpose, e.g. as restaurants, shops, hotels, etc.

In our Example 16, four abandoned traditional houses are filled by a natural accumulation layer, and, for some, a collapse layer resulting from the fallen roof. Even if all the natural accumulation layers are similar and result from the same long-term event, i.e. the accumulation of aeolian sand, each needs their own SU. It is critical that each SU is related to a basin of accumulation – in this exercise, each room represents one, and making the house itself one single basin of accumulation would be a major error. By so doing, it is easy to produce a distribution study of the finds by room, as well as to precisely locate SUs above and below accumulation layers.

The stratigraphic matrix of Exercise 16 is very 'horizontal', as all the accumulation layers are considered the result of a contemporaneous event. Nevertheless, it shows that the collapse is a post-abandonment feature, i.e. probably a natural event and not the result of any violent action.

Exercise 17 (explanation): North American pit house

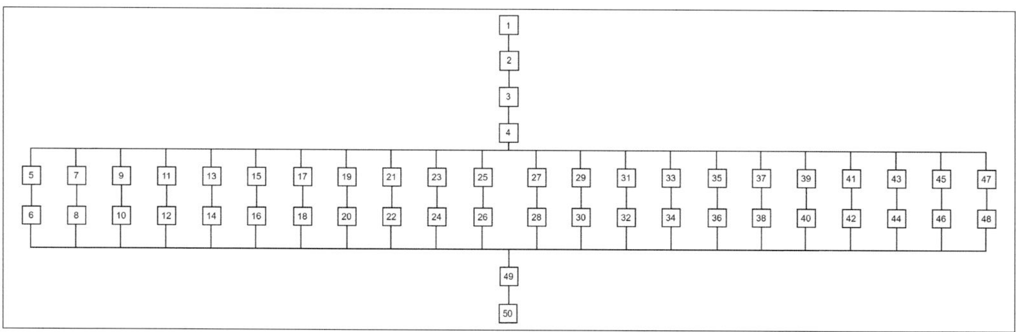

Figure 47: Exercise 17: matrix.

Exercise 17 presents what is commonly called a 'pit house', typical native architecture of the ancient southern USA. Of course, architectural units dug partly or completely in the ground are common around the world.

After the removing of the last layer of natural accumulation (SU 1), our archaeologist has to record the first natural accumulation layer (SU 2) that filled the house after its abandonment. Below SU 2, one finds an ashy layer (SU 3), probably a clue as to a general fire that destroyed the house. After removing SU 3, the excavator reaches some scattered remains of the original plastered floor (SU 4); here, the choice has been made to record them as a single unit (SU 4), even if they are unconnected. This is probably the best thing to do to avoid repetition in the recording on-site – something any archaeologist has to bear in mind so as to make her/his recording system efficient, not to say logical... Next, the fireplace (cut SU 10 and fill SU 9) inside the access corridor is recorded, as well as the long series of postholes used to support the wooden beams holding up the roof (SU 5 - SU 8, SU 11 - SU 48).

To take one example, posthole SU 5 - SU 6 comprises hole SU 6, originally made in the ground to take a beam, and a mix of decomposed wood and sediment infiltration (SU 5) that filled the hole after the beam had rotted away. Even if we lack further information, those postholes are all put at the same level on the matrix. It is important to note that they might not all be contemporaneous – some could be later additions made during phases of repair. Further analysis, e.g. C14 dating the charcoal from the posthole fills, could answer such questions.

At this stage, it is the time for our archaeologist to record the cut of the house – which, in a way, equates to its 'walls' and 'floor' (SU 49) – and the natural sediment in which the house was constructed (SU 50).

Exercise 18 (explanation): Artisanal quarter

This exercise shows an example of a small food processing unit, and the first layer to be recorded is a natural accumulation (SU 1) that covered two basins, a large one (SU 6) and a small one (SU 7), probably used to extract juice from fruit or other products, the liquid running from the larger basin into the small.

Even if the accumulation layers SU 2 and SU 4 inside the basins are similar to the general accumulation layer SU 1, and are the result of the same event, they have to be distinguished as they have different basins of accumulation. After removing the natural accumulation layers, our archaeologist needs to record the ash deposits (SU 3, SU 5, SU 9). Again, even if these three SUs represent a single event, e.g. a fire in this area, they need to be distinguished as they have different basins of accumulation.

SU 6 and SU 7 are the two basins, constructed inside a room of which only a stone wall (SU 8) is conserved, although the beaten earth floor of the building remains (SU 10).

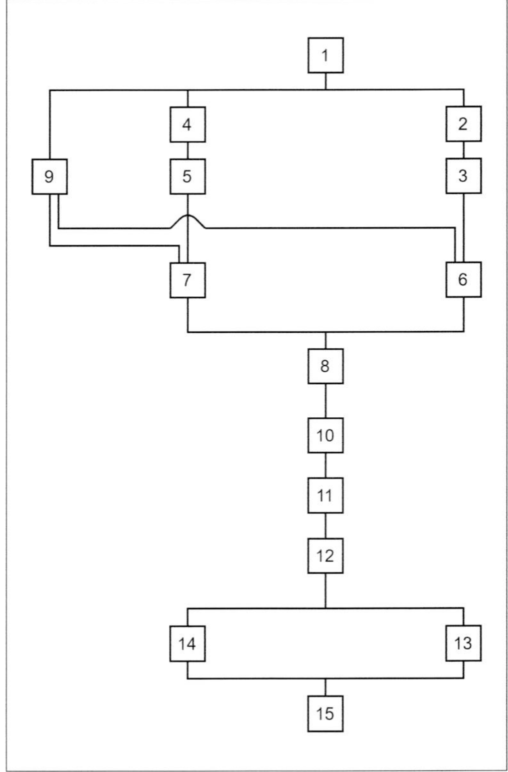

Figure 48: Exercise 18: matrix.

The structure was built over two earlier deposits (SU 11, SU 12). The removal of SU 12 enabled the team to find two column bases (SU 13, SU 14) placed directly on the bedrock (SU 15). These are the only remains of an earlier phase when some monumental buildings existed.

The matrix here has some tricky characteristics that are interesting to review. First, SU 1 is placed on top, but it is obvious that all the accumulation layers (SU 1, SU 2, SU 4) belong to a same time horizon. Although SU 1 existed for less time than the unit inside the basins (the upper interface of SU 2 and SU 4 is older than the upper limit of SU 1), it is correct to put it on top. Of course, SU 2 and SU 4 are paced on the same level. SU 3, SU 5 and SU 9 represent the ash resulting from the burning of the wooden upper structure of the room. As for the accumulation layers inside the basins, they are placed at the same level because they result from the same event. Here, it is interesting to see how our archaeologist has drawn a link between SU 9 and SU 6: it crosses through the link between SU 5 and SU 7, using a semicircular arc, meaning that there is no link between SU 9 on one side, and SU 5 and SU 7 on the other. It is the most common indication used to avoid misunderstandings when lines cross on the matrix.

The rest of the matrix is easy to understand. The two basins are part of the same feature, so they have to be put at the same level, and wall SU 8 is below them. While it was constructed on the beaten earth floor, it is above the floor on the matrix – something very rare in construction technique, which is probably a clue that this wall was constructed in a later phase of use of this space. Features SU 13 and SU 14 are combined by default as we have no indication of their chronological relationship. At the bottom of the matrix comes the natural, i.e. the bedrock (SU 15).

Exercise 19 (explanation): Pottery kiln

This exercise presents an example of a collapsed pottery kiln.

Our archaeologist has first to remove three natural accumulation layers (SU 1 - SU 3). We can see that these layers tend to be deposited in a horizontal manner as they have no restrictive basin of deposition (see 'Original Horizontality'). After the removal of SU 1 - SU 3, the excavator reaches the pottery production area, characterised by the remains of a pottery kiln (SU 4 - SU 7, SU 10), and a waste pit into which failed pots were consigned (SU 11, SU 12).

The following elements from the kiln are conserved: a part of the wall of the upper chamber (SU 4) and its retaining wall (SU 5); a small part of the furnace's perforated floor – 'dead plate' (SU 6); the central pillar of the combustion chamber (SU 7); and the combustion chamber cut (SU 10). Inside the combustion chamber, the kiln's destruction layer (SU 9) and a natural accumulation layer (SU 8) were recorded. The waste pit (cut SU 12, fill SU 11) was identified near the kiln: SU 12 cut into an earlier posthole (cut SU 14, fill SU 13), which was probably associated with the other posthole to its left (cut SU 16, fill SU 15).

All the features were cut into a thick layer (SU 17) deposited on the natural soil (SU 18).

The latest accumulation layers are naturally located at the top of the stratigraphic matrix. Below SU 3, we must

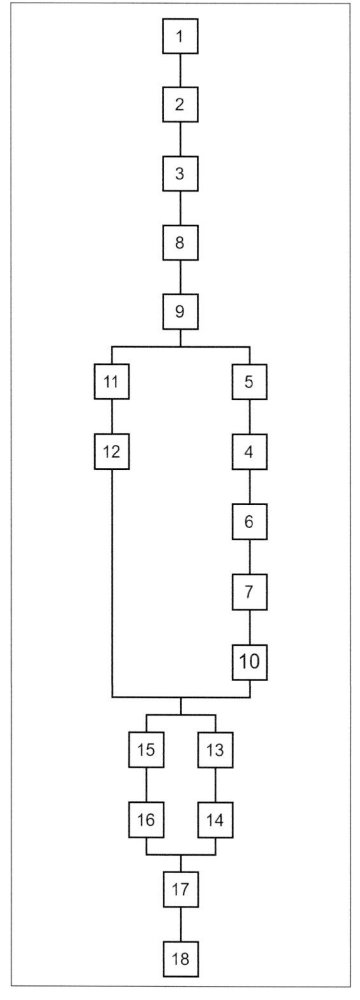

Figure 49: Exercise 19: matrix.

adhere to the rule of 'Stratigraphic Succession' by putting the SU chronologically closest to SU 3, i.e. SU 8, the natural accumulation that followed the destruction of the kiln. SU 9, the destruction layer of the kiln, is put below SU 8. It is important to note that all the relationships between SU 3 and the remaining parts of the kiln (SU 4 - SU 7, SU 10) can be ignored as they are superfluous. Indeed, the only important information here is that following the destruction of the kiln (SU 9) and the filling of its combustion chamber by initial natural accumulations (SU 8), other natural accumulations were later deposited over the site. The matrix then shows the period of use of the kiln (SU 5 - SU7, 10) and the waste pit associated with it (SU 11 and SU 12). Before the ceramic production area was constructed, some light installations existed from which only postholes are conserved: this is shown on the matrix by putting SU 13 - SU 16 below the last SU of the waste pit (SU 12) and the kiln (SU 10). Again, the superfluous physical links between SU 12 and SU 10 and layer SU 17 are not shown on the matrix.

Exercise 20 (explanation): Mediterranean mountainous site

This exercise looks at an imagined example of what could be a Mediterranean mountainous site featuring visible remains from different chronological eras.

On site, our archaeologist sees three distinct features: a commemorative stela (SU 1) on a high point; a series of agricultural terraces (SU 2 - SU 10); and a small temple (SU 11 - SU 20).

The stela is allocated the first SU, corresponding to its position on the site. The agricultural terraces have been constructed with walls ('terracing walls'), delimiting flat areas of agricultural 'steps', as it were, down the mountainside. There are four such terraces, i.e. A = SU 9, SU 10; B = SU 6, SU 7; C = SU 4, SU 5; D = SU 2, SU 3. Notice the presence of SU8, a collapse from terracing wall SU7.

For the temple, two collapse events can be recorded, i.e. SU 11 and SU 12. Although a single SU could have been allocated to record the collapses, it is more accurate here to allocate two, as the collapses are not similar, nor located in the same area, i.e. SU 12 relates to fallen masonry (SU 14) and SU 11 to a column. Three main architectural elements are also recorded, i.e. a wall (SU 14) and two columns (SU 13, SU 15). It is always best practice to allocate individual SUs for all architectural elements not physically linked. Time consuming as it may be, this is essential for any meticulous study of the construction process and chronology of the different architectural elements.

Our temple is built on an *euthynteria* (SU 19), and a *crepidoma* of three steps (SU 18 - SU 16), the last referred to as a *stylobate* (SU 16). Unlike the wall and columns, these step elements, all forming a single substructure, could have been included within a single SU if preferred. The substructure is built on an extensive levelled layer (SU 20) on natural soil (SU 21), below which is bedrock (SU 22).

In this example, where none of the features are buried, the different norms of stratigraphy become less relevant. However, this site still needs clear stratigraphic analysis. As we can see from the matrix, the construction of the agricultural terraces proceeds upwards. The collapse event SU 8 is assumed to have occurred following the disuse of the terraces. For the temple, the stratigraphy is straightforward: the collapse layers are the latest events, representing a phase of destruction/abandonment of the structure.

Subsequently, our matrix follows events from the latest to the earliest we can see, i.e. masonry, substructure, and levelling. SU 1, the oldest artefact on this site, comes above SU 21. SU 1 appears on the right, with no link to SU 20, to stress that it is not in the same vertical sequence as the other elements. However, placing it in the sequence between SU 20 and SU 21 would not have been a mistake.

The phasing of the site becomes quite clear to us: Phase I is represented by a commemorative monument; Phase II is the period of temple use; Phase III is the temple's abandonment; Phase IV is the very late use of the site for agriculture, by means of built terraces; and Phase V is the eventual disuse of the terraces.

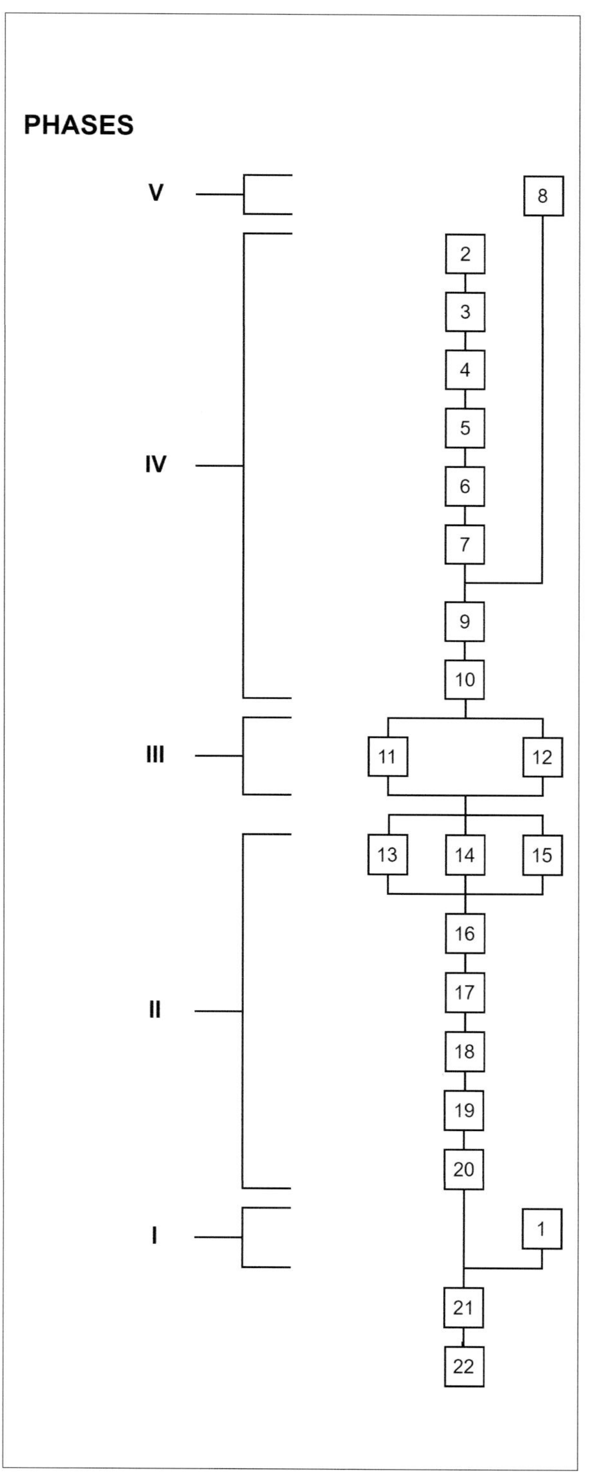

Figure 50: Exercise 20: matrix.

Exercise 21 (explanation): Prior unsupervised interventions at an archaeological site

This exercise represents a situation our commercial archaeologist needs to be prepared to face, i.e. starting an excavation after damage to a site due to initial unsupervised work. In this case it involves an intended foundation trench that has uncovered archaeological layers, i.e. several deposits (SU 1, SU 4 - SU 8), and a pit (SU 3) with its fill (SU 2).

The modern trench (SU 9) cuts almost all the layers (SU 1 - SU 8), so it appears at the top of the matrix. Beneath SU 9 the matrix follows the 'normal' sequence of the layer. It is worth noting that although the modern trench SU 9 is *physically* linked with many layers, in the matrix it is only linked with SU 1, i.e. the top layer into which it was dug. Indeed, it is the only relevant link for understanding the chronology of the site (see 'Stratigraphic Succession').

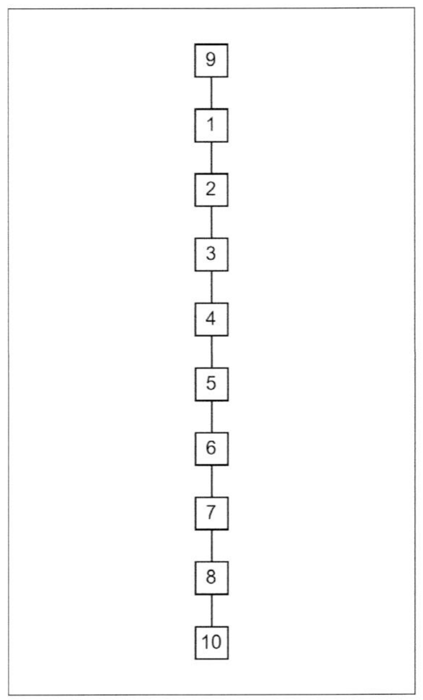

Figure 51: Exercise 21: matrix.

Exercise 22 (explanation): Anglo-Saxon building

This exercise shows in plan an example of an Anglo-Saxon 'post-in-trench' or 'long hall' building, a style of architecture that appeared in England *c.* 600 CE. Our example is characterised by a particular construction technique: the sinking of posts, or planks, within a *trench* – as opposed to *holes*, as in the more common posthole buildings.

Two large, 'U'-shaped trenches (SU 2, SU 4), with their backfills (SU 1, SU 3), form the general rectangular layout of the structure. The posts were sunk in the bottom of the trenches, and then the trenches backfilled. All around the building, some postholes near the trenches are the only remains of the buttress posts (SU 9 - SU 12, SU 13 - SU 18). The hole cuts are represented by SU 10, SU 12, SU 14, SU 16, SU 18, into which the posts were set, and the later fills of the holes by SU 9, SU 11, SU 13, SU 15, SU 17, resulting from the disintegration of the wooden posts and the accumulation of sediment. The three postholes (SU 19 - SU 24) inside the building mark an internal division. At the southern entrance, two large postholes (SU 5, SU 6 and SU 7, SU 8) are probably signs of a later doorway

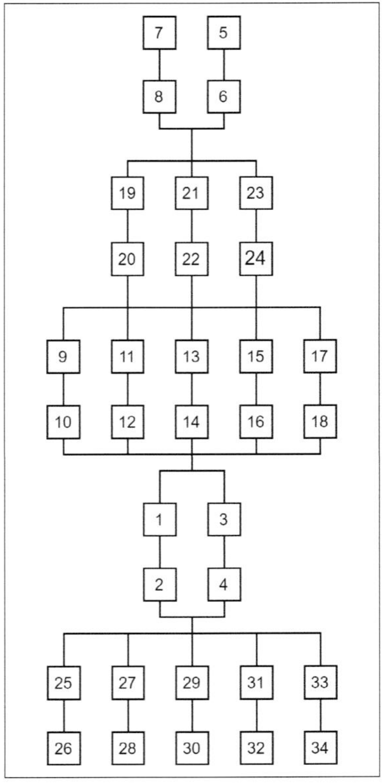

Figure 52: Exercise 22: matrix.

repair. This post-in-trench structure was erected over an earlier posthole building, of which only some postholes are now visible (SU 25 - SU 34).

Our matrix shows the different construction steps, i.e. the main trenches; the buttress postholes; and the internal N-S wall. The SUs of the earlier posthole building can be seen at the bottom.

Exercise 23 (explanation): Multi-period rural site

This exercise gives an example of a multiphase rural site, revealing activity from prehistoric to modern times.

After recording the last natural accumulation layer (SU 1), our archaeologist uncovers two stone alignments (SU 2, SU 3) used to mark property boundaries. These properties were constructed on agricultural soil (SU 6). Cutting into SU 6 and the natural accumulation (SU 7) was a robber cut (SU 5), presumably to remove stones from wall SU 14. SU 4 represents the backfilling of cut SU 5. Initially, a part of wall SU 14 was visible (i.e. above SU 6) on the surface when the inhabitants working on SU 6 decided to dig around the wall to take some of its stones.

Once SU 6 and SU 7 are cleared, we can record the collapse layer (SU 8) and an ashy layer (SU 9). SU 8 and SU 9 represent a destruction event – probably by fire – of the buildings associated with wall SU 14. Only a single wall in elevation was found, i.e. SU 14, with its foundation wall SU 15, the levelling SU 16 at the bottom of the foundation cut, and foundation cut SU 17. Cut SU 17 was made into SU 18, SU 19 and SU 20 and SU 21. SU 18 and SU 20 were a single deposit before being divided by SU 17. Near the masonry SU 14 - SU 17 we have pit SU 13 and its fills (SU 10 - SU 12). This pit was cut into SU 20 and SU 21. It is possible that SU 18 and SU 20 represent levelling, whereas SU 19 and SU 21 seem to be natural accumulation layers.

After SU 21, the excavator records deposit SU 22, discovering a small installation featuring two postholes (SU 23 - SU 24; SU 25 - SU 26) and three pits (SU 27 - SU 28; SU 29 - SU 30; SU 31 - SU 32). The three pits cut into layer SU 33 and the two postholes into layers SU 33 and SU 34. Below SU 33 and SU 34 comes the natural accumulation layer SU 35. This layer (SU 35) is overlaying two structures: a prehistoric tomb in the form of a small stone mound – or cairn – (SU 36 - SU 37), and an underground tomb cut into the bedrock (tomb cut SU 50, bedrock SU 51) and closed by a large block (SU 38). Inside the two funerary chambers, three stone sarcophagi were found, i.e. lidded, box-like containers for the deceased: right sarcophagus: SU 40 (cover), SU 42 (box), and SU 41 (skeleton); middle sarcophagus: SU 43 (cover), SU 45 (box), and SU 44 (skeleton); left sarcophagus: SU 46 (cover), SU 49 (box), and SU 47 and SU 48 (skeletons). SU 39 is a later infiltration from natural accumulation layer SU 35.

We can see that the deposits not restricted by particular or narrow basins of deposits have a tendency to be deposited horizontally, whether natural accumulation layers (SU 1, SU 19, SU 21, SU 22, SU 35), a destruction layer (SU 9), or poorly defined deposits (SU 33, SU 34). They could be dumps or natural deposits (see 'Original Horizontality').

Here we can identify some instances that seem to go against our rule of 'Superposition':

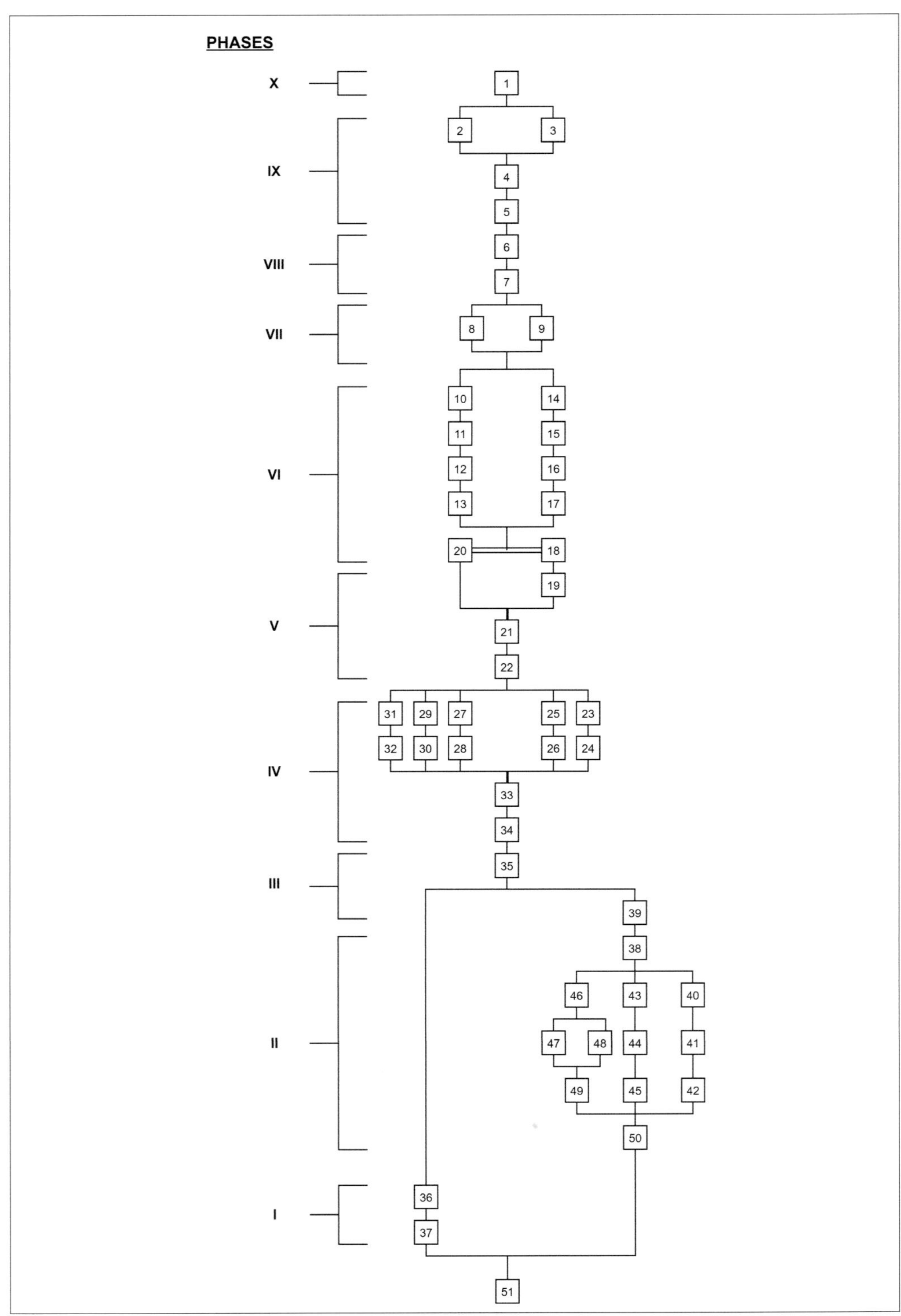

Figure 53: Exercise 23: matrix.

SU 2 and SU 3 are the higher units, but SU 1 was deposited later, so on the matrix this is shown by putting SU 1 on top.

SU 36 and SU 37 are higher than the SUs corresponding to the underground tomb, but, from the chronology, we know that it is an earlier structure and thus has to be put below the underground tomb on the matrix.

Even if SU 39 is below SU 38, it is above it on the matrix as it corresponds to a later infiltration.

Because SU 18 and SU 20 were, as already noted, a single layer before being cut by SU 17, they have to be linked by a 'same as' link on the matrix (see 'Original Continuity').

The robber cut and the wall give good examples of how the rule of 'Stratigraphic Succession' works. Even if cut SU 5 has physical links with SU 6, SU 7, and SU 14, only the link with SU 6 is shown on the matrix; the only valuable information in terms of chronology here is that SU 6 is later than SU 7. We can say the same for SU 8 and SU 9, which are physically linked with SU 14, SU 15, SU 20, and SU 10. The two non-superficial links are SU 8 + SU 9 with SU 14, and SU 8 + SU 9 with SU 10.

Before moving to the phasing, it is worth noting how the sarcophagi are recorded, i.e. with individual SUs for the lids, stone boxes, and the skeletal remains. It would be an error to give a single SU number to the box and lid together, the latter being a movable element.

The relative and absolute chronologies allow our archaeologist to group the units by phases.

- Phase I: This is represented by the funerary mound (SU 36, SU 37), dated to the prehistoric era, specifically between 7000 - 5000 BCE by its style.
- Phase II. Ceramic analysis from inside one of the sarcophagi allows us to place the underground tomb within the Roman era, thus SU 38, SU40 - SU 50 are grouped in Phase II. SU 39 is not placed in Phase II as it represents the abandonment events of the tomb, when a natural infiltration occurred, and thus cannot be considered part of the phase when the tomb was in use.
- Phase III. This is not an occupation phase but represents the abandonment of the area of the tombs and the natural accumulation that occurred subsequently.
- Phase IV. A phase grouping all the layers and features related to the early medieval period.
- Phase V. This is the abandonment process following Phase IV, characterised by SU 19 - SU 21.
- Phase VI. Represents 16th-/17th-century occupation, characterised by a large refuse pit and the remains of a monumental construction. As our dating only comes from C14 analysis of samples from the refuse pit, it is challenging to detail the chronology between the pit and the masonry. Here we have assumed that they were contemporaneous by putting them on the same level on the matrix.
- Phase VII. This reflects the destruction of the masonry of Phase VI.
- Phase VIII. This is the abandonment phase after the destruction of the area.
- Phase IX. Here we group all the events after the deposit of SU 6 – the robber cut and the field division.
- Phase X. This is the last natural accumulation layer after the disuse of the fields in the area.

Exercise 24 (explanation): Industrial archaeology

This exercise is an example of the type of lime kiln that could be commonly found *c.* the 17th/18th century in Europe. Industrial archaeology, sometimes linked with contemporary archaeology, can represent an important part of the work of any field archaeologist, especially in countries where relatively recent remains are involved – as in the USA and Saudi Arabia. The main issue is how 'archaeology' is understood: is it only the study of the past, or as a discipline like history that can also be used to study our present? Archaeologists who think that archaeology should not be linked systematically to the 'past' tend to consider their discipline as appropriate to the study of the material culture – i.e. any human production – whatever its chronology.

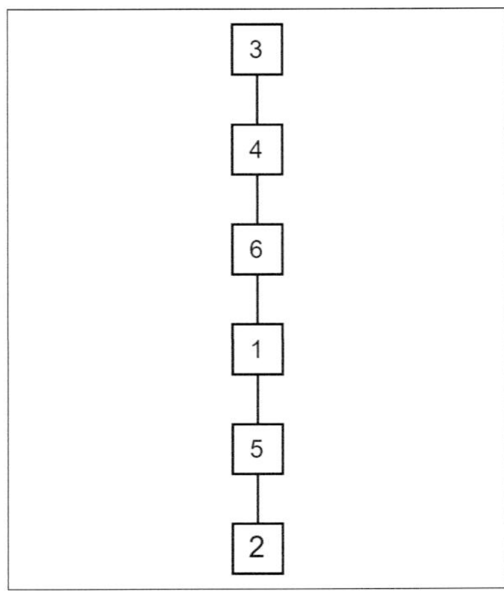

Figure 54: Exercise 24: matrix.

Our lime kiln features a hearth at the bottom, accessible through the vault SU 5, a bowl (SU 2), i.e. the part with flared walls, and the retaining wall SU 1. The kiln worked by placing limestone and combustible material inside the bowl and firing it; the resulting quicklime was then recovered from the bottom. After the abandonment of the kiln, the vault partially collapsed (SU 6), and the floor between the hearth and the vault fell away entirely, leading to the fill of the hearth and what remained of the limestone in the bowl (SU 4). After the collapses, a thin natural accumulation was deposited inside the kiln (SU 3).

Exercise 25 (explanation): Building archaeology

Exercise 25 is an example of building archaeology, i.e. the study of standing architecture incorporating a stratigraphic reading from an archaeological perspective. There is not space here to go into the method of building archaeology, simply that among its main goals is the subdivision into its smallest elements of each part of the building under investigation. The building archaeologist uses a unit system to isolate every element, similar to that of our field archaeologist, i.e. an SBU (Stratigraphic Building Unit). Each SBU defines a construction event (a wall, an opening, etc.), whether belonging to the same chronological period or not. This subdivision of built elements will hopefully provide a good understanding of the techniques and materials used, as well as a preliminary phasing of the construction of the building. Ultimately, the building archaeologist produces a stratigraphic matrix, similar in many respects to the one generated by our field archaeologist.

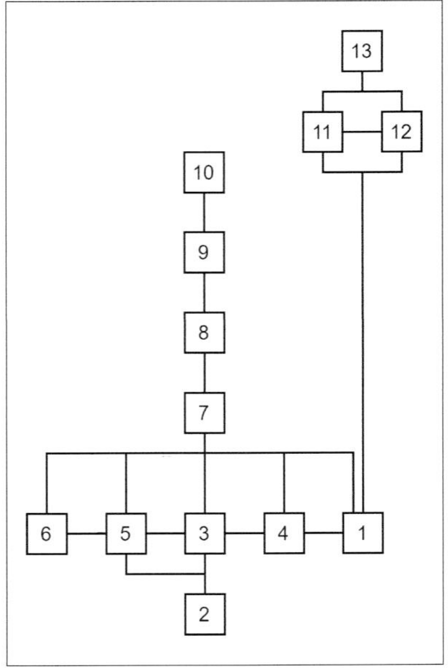

Figure 55: Exercise 25: matrix.

The facade shown in this exercise can be divided into SBUs according to the different elements visible. SBU 1, SBU 3 and SBU 6 are the different parts of the wall of the original facade, divided by the two doors SBU 5 and SBU 4. SBU 11 differs from SBU 1 by its stonework and bond. SBU 12 represents a well-built corner of the building.

The higher part of the facade includes SBU 7 - SBU 9. SBU 13 is recorded on the top of the building, on the right side. SBU 10 is the only (small) section of conserved plaster.

In the matrix, the arrangement of SBUs must show the different construction steps. The various elements of the original facade are put on the same level (SBU 6, SBU 5, SBU 3, SBU 4, SBU 1), representing as they do the same construction phase. SBU 2 was probably made just before SBU 3 and SBU 5 to compensate for differences in ground level. SBU 7 corresponds to a preparatory step in the fieldwork, before constructing the higher part of the facade (SBU 8). The intersection between SBU 8 and SBU 9 marks the level of the roof; SBU 9 being a course of stone construction on the roof. SBU 11 - SBU 13 were most probably constructed during a latest phase, when the house was enlarged. Generally, in building archaeology, elements at the same level and constituting the same feature are linked by a horizontal line, as we have done in this example.